JO ANN FAWCETT

THE PRINCE WAS WRONG

LEAVING THE NARCISSIST BEHIND

ISBN: 978-1-964619-02-6

DEDICATION

This book is dedicated to all those who have experienced narcissistic abuse. May you survive, heal, and move on from the difficult journey. Know that you are not alone. You deserve your best life. You have the strength to find joy.

TABLE OF CONTENTS

ACKNOWLEDGEMENTS

Thank you, Eric Wick, for being my best friend. For believing in me. For always telling me the truth. For telling me to keep writing.

Thank you, daughter Melissa Cole and sister Nancy Benton, for being my constant and much-needed support system.

Thank you, Erin Lund—Sunshine Editorial Services & Book Coaching—for planting the seed that led me to write this book.

Thank you to my therapist for your never-ending support.

Thank you, Sara Latourneau—Heart of the Story Editing—my intuitive book coach. Thank you for your expertise and encouragement. Our work together made the editing process easy. Thank you for your many reminders that is an important story to tell.

Thank you to my beta readers: Beth McDermott, Eric Wick, Christine Malek, and Dana S. Diaz. I appreciate you taking the time to read the book and provide valuable feedback.

Thank you to my publishing team at She Rises Studios. It was a pleasure working with you.

INTRODUCTION

Has your partner ever told you:

- You should have tried to be prettier.
- You started your business in my house, putting my needs on a back burner.
- I didn't support your project because it wasn't good timing for me.
- You sold big household items to pay for your project, putting all my efforts aside.
- You seem to be under the misconception that because I've tried to be nice about the situation you can have everything your way.
- Men don't tell their wives/partners why they love them; guys just don't do that. If I'm with you, that should be enough.

My heart goes out to you if you have heard things like these from your partner. Just as I have been, you might be the victim of narcissistic abuse.

When I heard statements like these from my ex-husband, I felt like I'd been slapped in the face. For twenty-plus years, I believed that we had a solid marriage. I was convinced we had great communication. I felt loved. It wasn't until I took a hard look that I realized that I was in a one-sided relationship.

No one deserves to be on the receiving end of a tantrum or verbal dressing-down—the vile words coming out of their partner's mouth or pen because they are furious that they are not getting their way. Verbal abuse is just as damaging as physical abuse. Both wreak havoc on one's well-being. Both cause a horrendous amount of stress. I may not have physical scars from this type of abuse, but I have emotional scars. I have been stressed to the max, to the point that my health has been at risk.

I am here to tell you that there is a way out of the situation. You can find the help you need. You can find the courage to stand up to your partner. You can leave if that's the best option.

I have been working with a therapist regularly for several years. I also moved out of "our" home. I now practice self-care. I am committed to having joy and adventure in my life. I am determined to associate with people who see me and my value.

My hope is that this book will show you that you are not alone. We can help each other as we share our stories, recognizing our strengths and weaknesses.

The prologue, which follows this introduction, is a letter to my ex that he will probably never read. If he ever does, he will not agree with it. He will not feel any remorse and he will not apologize for his behavior. Throughout the upcoming chapters, I will share examples of his narcissism. The relationship didn't start out bad and it was good for many years.

I realize now that I was living like a frog in the boiling water. I didn't know that I was in danger of losing myself until 20+ years had gone by. That does not have to be your story.

WHAT IS NARCISSISM?

Before starting therapy, I wasn't totally sure what narcissism was. I knew that my ex was extremely selfish (his words) and that my daughter used the word *narcissism* when speaking about him. But the light went on when I saw my future therapist's sign, "Dedicated to helping people recover from narcissistic abuse," printed over a beautiful heart. At that moment, I knew that narcissism was the type of abuse I'd been experiencing.

According to the Merriam-Webster Dictionary, narcissism is defined as "...extremely self-centered with an exaggerated sense of self-importance: marked by or characteristic of excessive admiration of or infatuation with oneself..."

Here are a few points from a good article that I read:

- "It's their needs that matter."
- "They don't believe in boundaries."
- "They have a hard time letting others shine."
- "They never seem happy for you."

(From "These are the Telltale Traits of a Narcissist," Lacey Johnson, *Oprah Daily*, October 7, 2022.)

I discovered that the narcissist in your life can be a partner, parent, child, sibling, friend, or even a colleague who bullies you. They will gaslight you and make you feel wrong because they always need to be right. They think that the rules don't apply to them.

Through my own experience, I learned that a narcissist does not see you as an equal partner. They try to isolate you from your family and friends. They belittle your creative efforts, especially if you aren't devoting yourself totally to theirs. They withhold compliments. They seem charming and wonderful to others and treat you differently when others can't see their behavior. They threaten violence and might be physically abusive. They are fiscally irresponsible.

Have you found these themes to be true in your relationship? If so, I invite you to keep reading.

PROLOGUE

Dear Asshole (aka Narcissistic Abuser),

When I met you, I thought I'd finally found a keeper.

After several failed marriages, I was certain that you were different from the other men. I was impressed with your intelligence and ability to have articulate, interesting, and often fun conversations. You're charming and funny. I could listen to your family stories for hours. Over time, I learned about your fascinating military career: the Army, the Navy, pilot, and top-secret intelligence work. I was proud of your honorable service as an officer.

As days and weeks grew into years, I put you on a pedestal. We could talk about anything. You opened my eyes to topics that I embraced as I soaked up new-to-me information about elementals, UFOs, aliens, space, and magic. You taught me to question everything and look beyond the public story. I couldn't wait to share this new-found knowledge and little-known history with everyone who would listen. I was honored to be your spokesperson, relating your military experiences at various UFO conferences.

What happened? How did we go from being best friends for twenty-five years to me feeling like the proverbial frog in a pot of boiling water? My co-dependent tendencies came out, just like they did during the abusive relationships with my former partners. I tried hard to please you, but in the process I lost myself and tunnel vision took over.

You have many great qualities, but you are extremely selfish. You always think you're right. You expect to always get your way. You expect everyone around you to follow your agenda because you have a way of making it sound like the best plan.

In the year leading up to the COVID-19 pandemic and shutdown, I started to wake up. I looked at my life and thought about what I wanted. I was sixty-five at the time and wanted to retire, but I was far from financially ready to do so. My life consisted of my work, visiting you in prison, doing research for your writing projects, and traveling to speak about your military adventures. A few times a year I would visit my daughter and grandchildren. I hated leaving you alone for the "big" holidays so at times I chose to spend them with you instead of the rest of my family (which was not an easy choice, as it made the family unhappy).

Around that time, I started writing a memoir about my other marriages and what I learned from each. I shared our story, too—how we met, the realities of being a prison wife, and your heroics. I wrote about how I changed my life, leaving a religion after thirty years of membership and finding new passions as I dove deeper into the world of UFOs, elementals, the paranormal, and magic. My spirituality grew. My intuitive gift blossomed. Most of all, the memoir showed that one can change their life and that it's never too late to change their path.

When I finally told you about the memoir, you didn't seem interested. So I stopped sharing it with you. You never asked about it. I heard later that you never talked about it with your friends. It wasn't until we were splitting up that you shared your true feelings about the project–that it took time and resources away from tending to your needs.

I lived in your very old family home for over twenty years. I paid for numerous expensive repairs and fallen trees. I never would have chosen to live there on my own, but we kept hoping that you'd be released one day and we would continue our life together in that house.

In the fall of 2019, I told you that we needed to have a plan for you to start paying for (or at least contributing to) the household expenses. After all, it was your family home and you have a great emotional attachment to it. Since you are in prison, the house is held as an asset of your trust and is not community property. You have always made me believe that you have money elsewhere and that we would be well-off financially once you got out. But, you have a life-without-parole sentence and there is no guarantee that you will ever be released. I should not have to work until I'm eighty or ninety, or until I just drop dead. As the thought of retirement seemed unachievable at that time, I said that by the fall of 2020 we needed to have a plan so that I didn't have to continue paying for everything. You seemed to be okay with my request.

I remember the day that I visited you in March 2020, not knowing that a week later all visiting would be closed due to the pandemic (and it stayed closed for a year). We were having a nice time. I told you about my recent trip to see the grandchildren. One granddaughter had told me that I needed different clothes. You agreed. I brushed it off but the way that you said it stuck with me.

During another part of that visit, I was joking that I was just your "cover wife," someone to visit you, take care of your needs, and provide clout if (or when) you needed to contact prison officials. Being married made you seem like the other married inmates. In truth, I felt like one of your "front businesses" that you ran as covers for your secret military operations. I didn't expound on my comment, and we didn't discuss it.

The only visits during that first year of the pandemic were awful video visits. We were still writing letters, but our in-person visits were the best way to really communicate about important family business. We could never be sure that our letters would get to each other. Plus, the prison staff reads and listens to everything, so it's never easy to discuss emotional or important topics in letters or occasional phone calls.

After a few months of isolation, I really started to wake up to the reality of our relationship. I didn't want to live in the house alone. I didn't want to pay all of the bills that went along with living in a big old house in an affluent neighborhood. I wanted to be appreciated, valued, and complimented on my gifts and ideas. I wanted you to see me as a desirable partner. Don't forget that I wanted you to develop a plan so that I was not the only one paying for all of the house expenses.

By late spring/early summer 2020, I decided to move out-of-state to live near my daughter. The move happened faster than I thought it would by a few months. An apartment became available, so I grabbed the chance to go. At the time, I didn't move because I was "leaving" you. My intention at the time was not to split up, but to take a break from the house and the isolation of the pandemic. Yes, it would have been nice to discuss the situation in person, but there were no in-person visits. I don't recall if video visits had been set up yet. Frankly, I don't think you would have understood no matter how I presented it.

You got my letter about the move much later than I'd hoped. You blew up and your nastiness came to the surface in a scathing letter. Without talking to me to understand my feelings, you launched into commando mode. You were convinced that I was leaving you. You wanted me to clear out of the house. It went downhill from there.

It's been a rough three years. We've both been hurt. My original intention was not to leave you–I told you so many times since I moved. We tried to patch up our relationship, but it kept imploding. I know that you expected me to move back to the house once regular visits were allowed, but that was not going to happen as I didn't want to be there in its state of disrepair. Of course, you blame that on me.

I tried being really open with you about what I needed in our relationship. Sadly, there was no empathy from you on that front and seemingly no desire to meet me halfway. I said that I would move home if the house was fixed up and you were released. Sadly, all my hope of us being together, and my love for you, has died.

What hurts the most is that now I feel that you pulled me into your life just to have someone who would visit you regularly and be a glorified secretary. Someone to buy your quarterly packages, send you writing supplies, pay for your subscriptions, and be the guardian of all the stuff at the house and whatever you sent home from prison.

Your tantrums, your gaslighting, and your bullying have been horrendous. You have acted like a spoiled toddler. I saw the mean side of you a couple of times during our prison visits, when you would give me stern lectures about things. I wanted to crawl under the table or become invisible, but you wouldn't let me leave the room. You wouldn't even let me cry in public. That would have embarrassed you.

I don't deserve such treatment. I used to think that we had great communication. I even bragged about it during podcast interviews. But I was so wrong.

So, here we are. I no longer let your abusive words hurt as much as they once did. I have filed for divorce. I am resigning from your trust. I am stopping all my payments for your house expenses. I am extricating myself from your life.

I am moving on to include joy and adventure in my life. I will retire. I will have fun. I will surround myself with like-minded people who see me for who I am and who like what they see–and that's something you never did.

Jo Ann

CHAPTER 1

HOW WE MET

The ex and I met in September 1997. My roommate came home one afternoon from visiting her husband, who was at the same prison as my ex.

"Jo Ann, I met this nice guy who's a friend of Sonny. He was visiting with his mom. He's smart. Would you like to meet him?"

I was impressed by the thought of meeting a smart guy, so I told her that I'd like to meet him.

"Great. I'll tell Sonny that it's OK for Bill to write to you."

Bill and I did start writing to each other. During those two months of correspondence, I learned that he was an only child and had grown up in a military family. His father had been in the Air Force. He had been in the Army and Navy. He had been a helicopter pilot during the Vietnam War. It wasn't until later that I learned of his other military duties. His letters and our eventual in-person visits were friendly, fun, and full of interesting stories. I enjoyed hearing about how his family had moved to England when he was seven, as his dad was stationed there for the Air Force. He told me about his friendship with a young English girl and how they would play for hours with the toads in the pond. He also told me stories of living in France and of his opportunities for delightful outings throughout Europe. I was enthralled to hear about the castles he visited and the history of such places.

I'm sure that I told him about my childhood, but his childhood seemed so much more interesting that I just let him do a lot of talking. I don't recall him asking me many questions about my background.

I learned that he was still fighting his legal case and he maintained that he was innocent of the first-degree murder charges against him. To this day, I believe that he is not guilty.

Two months later, during Thanksgiving weekend, we had our first in-person visit. I'd spent a couple of days with my family and would normally have stayed with them the entire weekend. I told them that I had a date to meet a new guy I'd been telling them about. They were not happy at all to hear that the date was to take place at a prison. My mom just looked at me like I was crazy, as her belief was that if you're in prison you must be guilty. I was convinced that this inmate was telling me the truth.

The prison was about an hour or so from my mom's house. I don't remember what we talked about on that first visit. I loved that he was a good hugger. He even asked if he could hold my hand before doing so for the first time, which I thought was sweet of him. Since we'd been writing for those two months, it felt like we had a good start and were already good friends. I felt very comfortable with him. We spent our time talking a lot and eating. I thought we'd never run out of things to say even though the visit lasted at least three hours.

We talked about our kids, our families, where we lived, the foods we liked, and our interests. He told me that he'd been in the US Army during the Vietnam War. As a child, his family had been stationed at numerous bases in the UK, Europe, and the US. I listened to stories about the places his parents took him to, about the history they taught him before they went. Through his stories, I learned about the customs of many places around the world.

When we met, there was visiting on Fridays, Saturdays, and Sundays, plus major holidays. I enjoyed his company so much that I wanted to visit him more than one day a week.

Positive Aspects of Our Relationship

At that early point in our relationship, the most positive aspect was that my horizon expanded. I learned new things about many topics by talking with this man. We discussed history, politics, spirituality, film, food, books, and people—more so than with anyone else, let alone someone I was dating. He was the smartest man I'd known. I loved bragging that we had better communication than I'd had in any of my former relationships.

He always appeared very confident when he entered the prison visiting room. He walked with his head and chest held high like a proud military officer. For the longest time, I smiled whenever I saw him, as I was so happy that we were together.

On top of all that, he always seemed happy to see me and spend time with me. He was polite and respectful. I knew he was writing to other women when we met, but I felt special as he obviously preferred to be with me. I learned that they did not live in the US, so it was easier to develop a long-term relationship with me as I lived nearby.

Eventually, I met his mom. She was charming like Bill and very ladylike. When I visited her at their family home, she was so proud to show me the family photo albums and various gifts given to them by overseas contacts. It was clear to me that the family had lived in and visited numerous places outside of the US just as he said. It was endearing to hear about her husband's military career and see the evidence in a photo album.

Marriage

We courted for five years. He was in prison that entire time as he'd been sentenced to life without parole. One day he proposed by saying that it would be a good idea to get married. Not very romantic, but neither of us cared about being married in general. I'd been married numerous times by then. We were both in our 40s.

At that time, lifers were not allowed to have overnight family visits, only in-person visits in the big visiting rooms with other inmates and their visitors. The fact was that a spouse has more clout than a girlfriend if one needs to contact the prison on behalf of their inmate. So marriage seemed like a good idea. I was honored to be given his grandmother's 100+ year-old engagement ring. We were married on my birthday, July 26—why not? Besides, he'd only have to remember one date for us, which I thought was helpful as he had numerous birthdays and anniversaries to remember among his family and friends.

I wanted to wear a red dress for the wedding just for fun, but couldn't find one. Instead, I wore a long black dress with a hot pink blouse; probably not the best colors for a hot July day, but I love hot pink. The groom was dressed in his best-pressed prison blues. Our wedding was held in a side room off the main visiting room used for legal visits. In attendance were my very pregnant daughter Jessie, former son-in-law Jim, Sue, a civilian friend of ours, and a few inmate friends. The ceremony was officiated by a pastor we knew who visited his son, but the ceremony turned out to be too Christian for our liking. Oh well. We exchanged rings, but there was no big fanfare. Our wedding cake was two Hostess cupcakes smushed together. No flowers. No music. I'd already had those types of weddings, so super simple was fine with me.

The wedding dinner was held at a local Red Lobster restaurant without the groom. It was just me, my daughter, my former son-in-law, and Sue. The honeymoon was me visiting him the next day and then going wine tasting and shopping on my own. Such was the illustrious beginning of twenty-plus years of marriage.

CHAPTER 2

WHY I DIDN'T SEE THE SIGNS SOONER

One would think that since this marriage was not my first, second, or sixth, I would have known much sooner that our relationship was in real trouble. I know there were signs, but I was so enamored with Bill that I swept those signs under the rug. As my daughter would say, "Did you need a sign-ier sign?"

So, what happened? What signs did I miss or ignore? I look back now and think to myself, "Duh!"

I enjoyed doing research for Bill's writing projects. I liked traveling and speaking on his behalf. As I shared his rather unknown information about the military space program, I felt like I was contributing to humanity's education. People were eager to hear more about this topic. I was doing important work.

I put Bill on a pedestal, for sure. I believed everything he told me—about his life, his military career, his legal case, his family, his children, and his supposedly substantial wealth. At one point, I saw a letter he'd received about a large deposit as payment for an assignment he'd completed. I've seen paperwork that included lists of businesses he owned or co-owned and of properties that he owned outside the United States.

I knew his mom, Margaret, before he and I were married. She confirmed many of the stories he'd told me, except for those about his military duties and about his children. Margaret was kept in the dark about her husband's and son's military duties as they were almost always classified. She knew they couldn't talk about the specifics of what they did or where they went, and I know that she didn't like not knowing. She also didn't like the amount of time they spent away from home and from her. If she knew about any of Bill's red flags, she never told me. She acted as if he were perfect.

There was evidence around the house—photos and souvenirs—that the family had lived outside the US, received lovely gifts from people in other countries, and had attended events overseas that most people would not have the chance to attend. I saw some of Bill's military paperwork. I saw letters to his children, and later from his grandkids when they were old enough to write. I read through his court transcripts and legal documents relating to his case. To this day, I believe that he's innocent of the charges for which he was convicted. And yes, I was in awe of who this family was.

In early 2000, I moved into Bill's family home with his mom and cared for her, as she had dementia. I helped manage her finances, took care of the house, drove her to medical appointments, and took her to visit Bill. Eventually, I arranged for her to go to a daycare center for seniors with memory problems. As her dementia worsened, I arranged for in-home caregivers so that I could work. A couple of years before she passed, I moved her to a nursing home so that she could receive the medical help and supervision that she needed. After two years, I brought her back to the family home and hired in-home help. She died peacefully in her home. I didn't resent being responsible for Margaret's care. Bill would not have been able to deal with it. As his wife, it seemed the natural way of things. In his mind, he'd lost his mom years before when her dementia became quite evident, so the 'loving wife' should just take care of it. Bill is a 'big picture' kind of leader. He has others take care of the minutia—a red flag I didn't grasp until much later.

Shortly after moving into the family home, I became friends with Sue, a friend of Bill's family. Sue warned me to not let him suck the energy out of me. She loved him like a brother, but she understood his personality well. Sue turned out to be right. I felt an energetic connection with Bill—a tingly feeling—whenever we held hands. On the flip side, my stomach would get tied up in knots when there was cause to worry about him through the ensuing years. When I first met Sue, I had no reason to think there would be problems in my relationship with Bill, but she was right about him, of course.

The first time I went to England to speak about his military experiences, she went with me. Bill had given me three lists of what to do while in England: must do, really try to do, and do these if there's time. We had rented a car (funny story for another time), so we had the means to get around, but we hadn't counted on the time it took to get to various places, especially when you don't know an area. People we met in England suggested places to visit, but Sue begrudgingly told them that we had to abide by Bill's list. Naively, I just assumed that he knew best how to capitalize on my first time in England, but I can see now that it was all about doing what he wanted. I was to visit certain places that he had connections with and take photos of such places—all to help with his big writing project. He was disappointed that we didn't do more things on his list even after I pointed out that there were fewer cars on the road when he was driving there years before and that I don't drive as fast as him. He expected that if he gave you "suggestions," they should be carried out.

Another of Bill's problems is that he is a man of secrets. It also takes him a long time to trust people. I get that. I understood that he was from a military family and that both he and his father had done top-secret operations for the military. So, I accepted that Bill couldn't tell me everything. But I still felt special, because I learned so much more about his secret stuff than his mom ever knew.

It took a while before Bill told me about his children and their mothers. He has at least twenty-five children that I know of with ten or twelve partners. He didn't share that information all at once. It came in stages. Some of it he told me outright. Other bits I read first in his writings about his military adventures. And other bits I didn't know until I read his will after we were married (crazy, right?). I do believe that the children and the women exist. Do I have proof of all of them? Not exactly. As I said, I've seen a few letters and photos, but I was never allowed to communicate with any of them, supposedly because one of his former partners hated me and the fact that Bill married me. I also have confirmation from a few mutual friends (and from some of my contacts in the spirit world—I speak with spirits through a channeling medium) that the women and children exist. Sadly, all I got from Bill was excuse after excuse as to why I couldn't meet his family.

Another red flag was the subject of his alleged wealth. Early on, Bill mentioned a large stock portfolio. The stocks, as well as several properties around the world, are all mentioned in his will. He also told me that he owned several businesses. I was impressed by this, but only to the extent that I thought it would be nice to date someone with money.

In addition, Bill gave me a few gifts in the early years before we married. Without even meeting me, his children and his former partners assumed that I was a gold digger, according to Bill. At no point did I ask for those gifts, nor did I stop working with the expectation of Bill supporting me.

Bill said he was advised by his lawyers or his family (I don't know who for sure) to draw up a prenuptial agreement before our wedding, but he decided against it. Because of this, he was allegedly cut off from a substantial "allowance" that he received from his investment earnings. Now I wish that we had done the prenup, but it probably wouldn't have mattered. To this day, I can't prove that any of that wealth exists. Although I am named as executor of Bill's estate, I have no documentation proving the existence of the stocks and property except for the family home that I lived in.

In hindsight, I wonder why we even got married. If there really was money to support us both and pay for his house expenses, why give up his allowance just so I would have the clout to speak with the prison officials if and when he needed me to do so? He seemingly trusted me enough to live in his house and know the names of his children and the stocks, but where was the proof? I was just supposed to take his word for it. It doesn't make sense.

Bill was also extremely cranky when he didn't get his way. I knew he was an only child and was rather spoiled. But over time, I learned that he expected everyone to follow his agenda and accept that he was always right. He liked his possessions. He liked feeling that he was in power. We often joked that it wasn't a good idea to "poke the bear," as he could get mean when we did.

Bill had a habit of discussing things by saying, "My thought is." I would usually think they were the best ideas as they always sounded so logical at the time. For example, we would daydream about when he'd be home. We talked about changes we'd make at the house. He would say, "My thought is that we'll change the living room into the master bedroom, including a master bathroom, and add on a new living room to the far side of the house."

When he convinced me to start a small publishing company, he assured me that it would be successful if I just followed his example from when he had a publishing company. I created good products but failed at marketing. I was not going to go up and down the Pacific coast as he had, selling the paper and magazine.

Until the last three years of our relationship, I'd only seen Bill's crankiness directed at me a few times. Once, I disagreed with him to the point that he got very sharp with me. I wanted to go to the bathroom to cry and compose myself. He didn't allow me to do so, as it would embarrass him if I was seen crying while leaving the room.

Another time I disappointed Bill, I became the subject of a very stern lecture. I felt like a punished child or student and about two inches tall. He gave me an intense look. His voice was quiet, and the tone commanded that I pay attention. His hand was on my knee or my arm. Again, I was not allowed to cry in the open visiting room. I just had to take it. I felt trapped sitting there in the chair. I felt like I did when my dad reprimanded me as a child. I was angry and embarrassed.

Until those last three years, I was mesmerized by Bill. I was so busy taking care of his needs and making sure our life together was as smooth as possible (at least to the outside world) that I didn't see that my needs were not being met. Caretaking is what I have always done. But once more people who knew us found out about the divorce, many were surprised. We had been so in love and had always looked perfectly happy as a couple. Oddly enough, though, several of my close friends and family told me that they had seen the signs all along.

CHAPTER 3

THE BEGINNING OF THE END

In the fall of 2019, I suggested to Bill—who was still in prison—that we come up with a plan for him to help fund the house expenses, as I'd been shouldering that responsibility since his mom passed away in 2004. After all, I was sixty-five and wanted to consider retiring from my full-time bookkeeping work. I couldn't do that if I was paying for everything.

I also suggested that we downsize a bit and purge some of the unnecessary belongings that none of our children would want. Bill agreed to my suggestion. Bill said that he'd start thinking of ways to downsize and how to fund the future house expenses.

At about the same time, I got the first inkling that maybe I wasn't getting all that I needed from our relationship. I felt overwhelmed with the financial burden of the house. I felt under-appreciated. I wanted more affection in our relationship. Until then, I hadn't really thought about it. Working on my first book nudged me to do so.

Fast forward to early 2020. The COVID-19 pandemic struck and changed the world. It certainly changed my life. I am not grateful for the pandemic itself and the lives lost, but I am grateful for some of the other results. I was able to do all my work from home and thus became more productive as I no longer drove to clients' offices and homes. I had more free time to work on my book.

And, I had time to look frankly at my relationship.

In March 2020, I attended a psychic development workshop taught by a friend of mine. It was held in person right before the pandemic shut things down. I signed up for the class because I wanted to learn how to use my intuition more fully. Bill knew about my interest in spiritual growth and psychic development. He showed interest when I shared what I learned in various classes. He didn't take my intuitive ability seriously, though, and that was disappointing.

I didn't know about it beforehand, but the last exercise of the workshop was for each person to cut the energetic cord with something or someone in their life that no longer served them. I chose to cut the cord with my relationship as it was at that time. I knew that changes needed to be made in addition to the house-funding issue, although I didn't know how to make those changes. It was never easy to talk about hard things with Bill, but I wasn't even thinking about divorce at that time.

The next weekend, Bill and I had an in-person visit at the prison, not knowing it would be the last one for a year. During the course of our visit, while we were chatting and snacking, I told him jokingly that my granddaughter had said I needed better clothes when I'd seen her a few weeks before the visit. He agreed. I also commented that I was a good "cover wife" so that everyone around him would think he was just a normal inmate while he continued to carry out his secret military involvement from prison since that's what he had me believing. He agreed. His agreeing to those comments irritated me, but I let it slide. Why couldn't he tell me that I looked fine in what I wore? Or, if he didn't think so, he could have encouraged me to splurge and buy different clothes. Why couldn't he appreciate me for going to visit week after week?

We were looking forward to a two-day family visit the following weekend—almost 48 hours in a small apartment on the prison grounds for the two of us to share some quality time outside the regular visiting room. A couple of days later, the family visit was canceled, and the regular visiting program was closed—both due to COVID.

Until the COVID-19 shutdown in March 2020, Bill and I had no memorable discussions about funding the house. We continued to write daily, but there remained the problem of not receiving all of each other's letters. Plus, the mail was always read by prison staff, so we were not completely comfortable sharing all of our thoughts, feelings, and important information. Many months into the shutdown, the prisons instituted video calls in lieu of in-person visits. They helped as we could see each other, but it was difficult to hear one another and not be distracted by the conversations of the inmates on either side of Bill. Plus, the guards monitored the calls. In 2022 the inmates were given tablets, so we were able to send email-like messages back and forth, but like our letters, each message was read and approved before being sent to the inmate.

As the pandemic shutdown continued, I settled into the routine of almost 100% isolation except for grocery runs. Eventually, a friend began delivering groceries to me. I did all of my client work from home. I paid the bills. I talked to my daughter and sister by phone. I listened to the large trees creaking and swaying loudly when it was windy. I constantly worried about when the next tree would fall over—or, at the very least, when the next big limb would crack and land on the neighbor's property, as they had many times before.

During that time, my daughter, Jessie, sister, Lee, attorney, Mary, and various friends encouraged me to stop paying for all the house expenses. In fact, they insisted and kept on me about it. There was always going to be another tax bill and another big repair needed. I couldn't continue to pay for that old pricey house in Northern California if I ever hoped to retire. No one can afford a property like that on one income. The pressure of the huge responsibility had also started to affect me physically and emotionally. I gained weight. I didn't go walking as much as before, and I became depressed.

My acupuncturist even saw the effects of the stress as she worked on me. Danielle would report that my liver, kidneys, and adrenals were very unhappy. I don't understand how all that works, but I knew that my body was unhappy, as she put it. My digestive system often felt distressed. My legs retained fluids. I had headaches. My energy levels were low.

That spring, my daughter encouraged me to move to Portland, Oregon. That way, I could be near her and her children. I would be part of their quarantine bubble so that I wouldn't be isolated. The seed was planted. I wondered if there were affordable apartments in her neighborhood that allowed three cats. I wondered how Bill would react. I worried about the logistics of such a move. Who would watch the California house while I was gone? My initial intention was that it would be a temporary solution while we all waited for COVID to end. Of course, my daughter hoped that it would become permanent.

I realized that such a move would strain my resources even more as I would be paying for two households, but I decided to go for it to improve my mental health. All I needed was a small apartment for the cats and me. My goal was to move in November 2020.

Finding a landlord who would accept three cats, not charge a high pet fee, and offer reasonable rent was not easy. My daughter and I both looked online for suitable apartments in her neighborhood. There were several affordable options, but most only allowed two cats. She looked at one for me that was to become open in July. It was in an older building and was not as well cared for as I'd have liked, but I decided to take it. My moving date was then pushed up to the end of July.

I planned to pack only the most needed belongings, send most boxes by UPS, and take a few things in the car, along with the cats and my luggage. A mutual friend who had lived at Bill's family's house for several months also agreed to return to the house and act as caretaker for the property. He had been working in Los Angeles, but that job ended. So, I thought I had all the bases covered. I fully intended to return when the pandemic ended, thinking that Bill and I would have time to work on our relationship and fix up the house.

The thing is, Bill and I didn't have a chance to discuss my move before I left California. I chose to not write about what I was planning until it was more certain. Frankly, I didn't want to read any of his backlash about it. I didn't want to hear his opinion or his alternative solutions to convince me to stay in the house. I knew that was what he'd do. I wrote to Bill when I was approved for the apartment. I assured him that it didn't mean divorce. I just needed to get away from the house and the isolation. Unfortunately, he didn't get my letter as quickly as I'd hoped.

Bill's initial reaction was like a bomb exploding. He went ballistic. Instead of reaching out to me first to discuss the sudden change, he went into commando mode. He wrote to me that he'd contacted his family, giving them a new reason to dislike and distrust me. He also started organizing plans to protect his belongings. He assumed that I was leaving permanently and that our marriage was over, so he demanded that I get all my stuff out of the house immediately. I don't know why, but I was shocked to read such rage from him. He hadn't been that angry with me for years. Yes, I should have prepared him for the probability and then the reality of the move. I just didn't want him to talk me out of it. It was one way I could stand up for myself.

After his appalling response to the news of my move, Bill calmed down a bit. His letter, dated July 16th (which didn't arrive until August 9th), said that he just wanted to say hello and make "an attempt to keep the doors of two-way communications open" instead of expressing the darkness that he was feeling. A few paragraphs later, though, he resumed his subtle gaslighting:

> I do honestly hope you are finding your new path to be the one that is good for you. One of us may as well get close to being happy . . . and it's rather clear at this point that it's not going to be me. Anyway, next week I'll try to put a few basic ideas together to try and work with your new demands. I hope you find joy and happiness in your view of the future, and in the directions you have

taken. I sincerely wish I could be there with you and perhaps remind you of the Magic left in your world that you seem to have put aside.

Little did Bill know that the magic in my life had come more alive since I'd moved. He seemed to think that I would only feel its presence if I lived in his home. That is definitely not the case. I'd resumed my practice of regular walks in my beautiful neighborhood and the nearby parks. I have a gratitude practice. I set intentions. I journal. I listen to my intuition. I have a special connection to animals and energy beings. I communicate with spirit guides.

As we tried to move forward, Bill expressed good wishes in his August 2nd letter:

I'm looking forward to hearing all about your trip, the new place, and how you like the new area up there. Hopefully you can relax a little and not have the problems you seemed to be facing down here. Maybe being around the kids more often will keep you amused. I sincerely hope this is a positive change for you.

His letter dated August 6th also had some positive thoughts. He said, "Believe it or not, I'm pleased that you are happy and hope that the next few months near your family prove to be positive for you."

Clearly, the continued COVID shutdown had a negative effect on most, especially the incarcerated. Bill noted in his August 14th letter, "A big part of the small joy-of-life that remains for me has been removed by the loss of our visits. Six months with no visits is apparently making me very short-tempered and mean (according to some people here)."

Although we didn't discuss my book project much, he noted in his August 30th letter: "I'm very happy your book is going so well and look forward to seeing it someday."

As we moved forward after my move and I kept pressing him for answers about our relationship and the house, I would get letters from Bill with comments such as these from a letter dated September 8, 2020:

> Got several of your letters tonight. I am hard-pressed to say much to you on several topics that you keep pushing me on, so let me give a stock answer for the moment. Yes, I am trying to work out ways to pay some of the major house bills. It takes me time for every step. I can't afford mistakes, so researching the options when you refuse to help or take any part in the effort means it is going to take me a few months.

As you can see, Bill criticized me for not helping him look for funding options, but I did help him. His family and I investigated various reverse mortgage and loan options. The fact of the matter was that the house was owned by Bill's irrevocable trust—not by any one family member—and banks do not lend to trusts. One bank suggested that the trust quit-claim the house to me so that I could take out a loan for the funds needed to remodel the house. Bill and his family would never have agreed to that, though, and I was not willing to take on more debt. Also, the problem with a reverse mortgage is that a lender expects the home to be owner-occupied and not used as a rental. Well, the trust was the owner, and the trust couldn't live there. I certainly didn't want to live there in its state of disrepair.

Bill hoped that a friend would fix up the house to make it rentable and sell a few of Bill's things to provide money to pay the bills. Bill sent me a list of what to keep and what to sell, stating that it was "a few more examples of how far I'm willing to bend to try to keep this ball rolling." He had always been very attached to his stuff. Yes, I knew he'd been in prison for many years and was afraid of losing everything, but downsizing is imperative as one ages, in my opinion.

Now, how old is this house? Well, it was built in 1912. So, it's OLD. And from 2004 to May 2023, I paid the property taxes, the insurance, all repairs (major and minor), gardening, major tree work, appliance replacements, and, of course, the utilities. I paid over $100,000 during that time. To fix it up enough to rent would have cost at least half a million dollars.

Over the course of our marriage, I had suggested minor remodels to make the house more comfortable—a bathroom upgrade and new kitchen flooring, for example. Bill had always put it off, saying that he had plans to remodel the house when he got out of prison. So only things that became emergencies—like leaks in the roof, fallen trees, a new water heater, a new section of sewer pipe, and a new furnace—were fixed. As I wrote this book, the house still needed major sewer pipe work, a new roof, electrical re-wiring in many rooms, a kitchen remodel, ceiling repairs, and more. Anyone looking to buy the house would need to gut it or demolish it and rebuild it.

As I've said, the house is old. I did not cause it to fall apart. Plus, it was full of Bill's stuff, his parents' stuff, and my stuff. There wasn't enough room for all of it, and I never felt like I could fully move it or make it feel more like my home. It felt more like a daily reminder of Bill's childhood home, and I didn't want to live in it. Most couples want to put their own style into their home; I never felt like I had that opportunity.

After being in Oregon for about a month-and-a-half, Bill's letter from September 13th noted:

> Clearly a lot to talk about, as it is becoming sadly clear that if we don't get back on the same page pretty soon when it comes to working with each other rather than for our own path, this relationship is going to wander away from both of us. Believe me, I get the idea you want to dump my house. I've heard from you for months on the subject. Your realtor friend is wrong—this is a stupid time to sell, and not in a condition to sell it. Nor is it smart for me to sell it, as it means that if I get to Board in the next few years I won't have any ties to the community, and thus ruins my chance at a parole; not to mention a dozen other reasons I have no intention of selling it. There are several options, but I need you to stop pushing me to sell the place!

I disagreed with Bill about selling the house. Quite frankly, the real estate market in that county was booming during the first year or so of COVID. People wanted to move out of the big city nearby and have more space, as they were working from home due to the pandemic. The statistics provided by my realtor friend encouraged me that the timing was perfect for selling the house. Alas, such was the pattern of our relationship. Unlike what I used to think, we really didn't agree on so many important topics.

CHAPTER 4

OCTOBER THROUGH DECEMBER 2020

I started working with a local therapist in September 2020 after seeing her sign in my neighborhood stating that she specialized in cases of narcissistic abuse. As we began our sessions, I learned more about the classic behaviors of a narcissist. Bill's nature and behavior matched the definition of a typical narcissist. I now had a term to describe his "extreme selfishness." Working with the therapist was one of the best decisions I made as I navigated the murky waters of the last years of our marriage.

Little did I know then that isolation of the abused is a common pattern with narcissists. If I only listened to Bill and believed what he told me, we would be fine—in his eyes. And for the longest time, I agreed with him. After all, we were getting flak from both of our families, so of course we shouldn't listen to them. I only wish I had heeded their warnings sooner. As I worked on this book, my daughter told me, "I wanted to shake you for years." My sister said, "We tried to tell you for years not to stay with him."

My goals and questions—or my "demands," as Bill saw them—were to find more equal ground in our relationship, discuss our feelings honestly in more depth, and figure out the financial piece of the house. I brought up these topics in many letters as they were important to me, and his answers were slow to come. I realize that things don't happen quickly when one is in prison.

Plus, he had a job, activities, and other things weighing on his mind and occupying his time. I get it—the man had a life. But I had a life, too, and I was anxious for answers. I wanted to fix the relationship or move on.

I was also worried about whether I'd be able to retire. I hadn't prepared adequately on my own. I hadn't started a retirement fund until I was sixty. I was hoping that he'd be out of prison sooner and that he'd take care of us as he had said he'd be able to do. I certainly would have been fine with semi-retirement, doing part-time work to help with the family finances. Now I was facing the fact that he would probably never get out of prison and I would have to keep working full-time until I dropped. This terrified me.

Numerous issues came to light as I started pondering the true nature of our situation. I want to be in a loving, committed relationship that is an equal partnership. I want to know why my partner loves/likes me. I want him to see me as a unique, wonderful person. I want to feel like more than a secretary who just provides office supplies, fulfills research requests, and acts as a weekly companion even when it's admittedly fun. I want to feel like my needs are being met. I want my opinions to matter. I want to feel supported when working on my own creative projects that are important to me.

But with a narcissist, it's their way or the highway. They believe they are always right. They believe they have the best solutions to every problem. If you are not in alignment with their agenda, you're in the wrong. There is no wiggle room. And they don't like to compromise, even if they say that they are willing to do so.

As Bill and I plowed through the rough times after I moved out of state and brought up my issues, I saw a very unpleasant side of him. Our life together up to this point had been fairly smooth, as I had never made big demands of him. I worked, took care of matters regarding the house, visited him, and took care of his less expensive physical needs relating to prison life (an occasional supplies package, stamps, writing supplies, etc.). He was focused on his life, his routine, his creative projects, and his children and grandchildren. How dare I upset his routine?

From his long letter dated 10-6-20:

> Mail last night brought a number of your letters demanding my attention and direct communications on a number of subjects. I've started this several times over the last several weeks, only to rip it up as finding the best path without getting rather dark hasn't been easy. Consider some of the things you have said over the last months, and how deeply they have wounded me. You have been very clear on a number of points and made it very open that you have a long list of problems that need to be addressed and resolved without much consideration of my point of view. I get it. For seven months both of us have had only voices and advice that feed "our side" of the story, with little support for the continued working effort to save the union—and thus it has suffered. Now we are both willing to snap and look for the flaws in each other, thus allowing the poison to flow and the health of the wonderful and fun relationship we used to enjoy to fall apart. That hurts me as much as anything, and I wish I could find some way

to save that working relationship—but the way you sound, it may already be too late.

One of my complaints was that I felt like his secretary, as there were often tasks for me to complete for his creative projects. For many years I loved doing that even though it was time-consuming. As my own business grew, I admit that I had less time for his projects. I was feeling unappreciated as a whole.

Also from the October 6th letter:

> As for you being nothing but a secretary, considering how little I've asked of you along those lines in years I hardly know how to react to that. Did I enjoy being able to have you help with such things from time to time? Of course. Did I believe that you wanted to help and be an active part of my creative efforts? Yes, I did. I never thought of you as a secretary. I thought of you as a loving wife who was trying to help me build something together. Since you established your own business, and more so since you've been working on your own book, any such help that I've needed I've asked my daughters or friends to handle so you didn't have to. I think it's pretty clear that the success of the relationship has nothing to do with any idea of you being a "good secretary." You seem to be convinced that you take care of a lot of stuff for me, and that's why I keep you around. I might point out that all the travel and lecture series stuff is something you enjoy and do for yourself. You haven't lifted a finger to help with any part of the legal fight— the kids have helped with all that for the last five years.

Any time I've asked for a bit of help with business ideas on any level I've been met with negative results for a decade, so that can't be it. So, apparently, I care about you for reasons other than any hope of you being a "good secretary."

Mind you, I don't recall being asked to help with the legal fight in the last several years and I did not have money for lawyers. And while I had done some research to help Bill with his business ideas, I knew my limitations. What he needed help with were tasks that were not in my wheelhouse.

He had wanted me to pitch one of his fiction books that I published to a well-known literary agent in Los Angeles. Marketing has never come easy for me, and I didn't know how to pitch to agents years ago. Once the agent heard that he was in prison and wouldn't be available to do his own interviews or a book tour, all interest in Bill as an author disappeared. I got his book into a few bookstores, but it took a lot of time and effort just to place them on a consignment basis.

Later, he was part of a creative writing group at the prison. They wanted a book produced and a website developed to showcase their creative efforts. I put together a booklet (I already knew how expensive self-publishing was) and started to set up a website. Bill was supposed to send me money to cover the beginning expenses. He never did.

Bill also had an idea for a video game. I researched various companies that might be interested in new ideas, but I was not the person to pitch a video game that I knew nothing about.

It was important for me to know why Bill loved me. I thought that was a reasonable request to make of him, but he would never answer me. As I once asked, he responded in his October 6th letter:

> As for me not being able to articulate how I love you—I have never suggested that I am a fountain of loving expression. You knew that when you entered this relationship. I try to send love cards and a number of other small efforts to let you know you are loved, but apparently, they are not enough. I wasn't aware that standing by you for 22 years amounted to nothing but rubbish. Even if I am reluctant to be overly gushy because of the environment that I'm in, one might have thought that my efforts had earned more than that. Yes, I do see that you need more emotional attention—I could use a lot more emotional support myself—and I am more than willing to try to pay more attention to articulate how I love you in the future. That's hard to do when nearly every letter has several hurtful digs in it for me to deal with while I'm trying to write a reply.

So, for the first two years or so of the pandemic, Bill and I tried to keep our marriage together. We continued to write letters to each other regularly, even though many letters never reached the intended party. We mailed them but sometimes they never made it past the mailroom staff who controlled the incoming/outgoing mail. We sent lovely cards to reassure each other of our love and our intention to stay together. Bill often expressed how much he missed me and our weekly visits; he even said that our visits made him a nicer person. He wasn't as outwardly romantic as I'd have liked, but he tried to show me through his cards, letters, and cooking for me at the family visits. Thankfully, during COVID, family visits were reinstated, and in-person visits were eventually allowed as well, albeit with new restrictions.

Even though it was painful to read the letters Bill wrote after I moved out of state, doing so confirmed my decision to find my voice and use it when communicating with Bill. After the October 6 letter in particular, I wrote to him about my desire to have a more equal partnership with him. I also wrote, "One's work is not more important than the other's when it comes back to the family. One's needs are not more important than the other's needs." He didn't receive it until November.

On 10-29-20, Bill sent me a lovely, romantic card with an island scene at sunset, including palm trees and the ocean. Inside he wrote:

> How would you like to go to an island with trees and sand that looked as bright and warm as on this card? Had to send this to my wife who wants more romance in our lives. I can't think of too much more in the romantic field than the two of us on the sands of a South Pacific Island—far away from all the people who keep tossing their words into our relationship to either drive us crazy or slowly drive walls between us. This is a reminder that we can find places and paths to happier times. I'm reminded how happy we can be in a prison visiting room or a family visit apartment.

By November 11, Bill was talking about one of his daughters doing some research into selling some of the cars that he allegedly had in England. That would have indeed solved the financial stress of the house expenses. Nothing came of this plan as you'll read in the coming chapters.

Being incarcerated is stressful enough—and Bill shielded me from the worst of it—but being incarcerated during the pandemic compounded the stress. I get that. Yet it didn't change the fact that, as a narcissist, Bill didn't like to be pushed about subjects he didn't want to deal with, as he showed in this letter dated 11-14-20:

And rather than any support from you, I get more demands to revisit these questions that you've been locked on for months, and that oddly when I've tried to answer seem to either not have reached you or made no impression if they did reach you (even though I've suffered the slings and arrows of people here for months concerning the topics at hand). If you are trying to build a collection of statements to twist and use against me in a divorce action—as both the people here and some members of my family believe—so be it. I've done nothing but try to make you as happy as I could under the circumstances at hand, and if you are now trying to twist all that around, so be it. I'm too tired and too hurt and fed up to hold much back at this point.

The question of why I've loved you. What man ever has to answer such a question? Why does anyone love anyone? Why do you love me? Have you ever thought about how you would answer such questions, or how it would make you feel if I asked such things and made it clear that I was asking them because I was suddenly insecure about our relationship and whether or not you were sincere?

It might seem that I didn't give him time to reply, but we were writing on an almost daily basis to each other. So thoughts, comments, plans, questions, and frustrations were constantly being exchanged while we also tried to include tidbits about our usual daily goings-on. We actually had a phone call on November 15. I was able to tell him that I hadn't received some of his answers, so he tried again in his next letter to me dated November 15-16.

In his reply dated November 15-16, Bill answered many of my questions:

> You defend the point that you never said you were leaving me, and only my family and I surmised that, or assumed that was the direction you were heading. Well, you may not have put that statement into text, but how any of us weren't to draw that as a conclusion is beyond any rational person. Think about it. After telling me to support the house myself if I want to save it, and that you are leaving the place for me to come up with how to fix the place and pay the bills—how is anyone going to look at that? What, you think I'm going to come up with all the money and methods to save my home after you walk away from it—and then what? A few years from now when everything is fixed up and paying for itself you're going to just walk back and move back in? Not only did you walk out and leave our home all but empty, and unprotected, with repairs needed and bills to be paid, but you refused to get your stuff out so that I could

have Tom fix it up and rent it! You've put every roadblock you can think of in my way to slow me down and make saving my home next to hopeless. And you don't see how anybody on my side of the action looks at your moves and wonders when the next ax is going to fall?

When I wrote my first book, a memoir, I waited for quite some time before bringing it up to Bill. After all, he was the prolific writer in the family. I had already published two of his fiction books. He was constantly working on creative projects and teaching writing classes at various prisons. What could I produce that would measure up to his excellent works?

I poured myself into it and allowed myself to be vulnerable, sharing my journey. Most everyone who read my first book enjoyed it. I sent a copy to Bill. He said he was very happy about my new book. Once he received a copy, he said it was very interesting and nicely written. "Reads well, with an easy flow and a good pace. I have no complaints. I am very impressed, and very proud of your little work of art."

As I learned to assert myself more with Bill, I asked him why he didn't support my book more. In the November 15-16 letter, he said:

> As far as your book is concerned—I've told you I think it's great that you have written something, but your story about a half-dozen husbands at this moment is not one that helps me in any way. Your timing, in fact, could not be worse. As I try to work for my commutation, your new tell-all about this gathering of mistakes doesn't make

me look good or feel special. I've said nothing about it because I don't have anything to put forward—the last thing I need right now is for it to come in here for these people to read and have yet another thing to use against me. No, I don't begrudge you for working on your book. Originally it sounded interesting as a look at a woman's trek under difficult conditions to a positive path in a relationship. When it turned into a tell-all about six husbands and all that's bad about loser men, I saw nothing but trouble coming my way. I don't expect you to stop the project but forgive me if I'm not real excited about it.

All Bill could think about was how my book affected him. I actually painted a very positive picture of him in that book. I described our relationship in glowing terms compared to the first six husbands. At the time of its writing, I was still very much in love with him. I was honest in my assessment of what it was like being a prison wife. I will always think of him as a military hero, just not a good partner.

His November 15-16 letter continued as he commented on my desire to have a more equal partnership.

I note your point that "as spouses, we are meant to be helpmates and equals. The loving husband and wife should support each other. One's work is not more important than the other's when it comes back to the family. One's needs are not more important than the other's." All true, to a point. At this moment, I don't see a whole lot of equal support, but you'll have to forgive me as I've had to stop everything I was doing for two months to try and figure out how to save the house and pay the bills. You know, a lot of women would consider a few bills and a bit of upkeep an equal load to carry when the husband has provided a lovely home. As far as retirement fears and when I expect that you will stop paying all the bills—as has always been the plan and the understanding, as soon as I'm out of here, and can access my investments and get reorganized (and provided you haven't left me). I have always expected to not only take over all of the bill paying (so much for equal, right?), but provide both of us with a very comfortable life. I'll be the one who keeps working and keeps active and building. I'll be the one who works around the house, takes care of the cars, and all the rest of life in general. I'll also do a lot of the small-time upkeep on the house and other stuff because I hate having things look rundown or unkempt. Nor has any of this ever been a secret. It has always been part of the long-range plan. Why you suddenly got paranoid and went off on this "defend Jo Ann" tangent has more to do with the alone time thanks to COVID-19 and private stress than any sort of real threat to your long-range well-being.

Believe me, considering the COVID-19 changes, I get your desire to move and be closer to your family. You could have done that without any of the current drama if you had worked with me to rent the house so that there wasn't the threat of the loss of a valuable asset. You want an "equal" relationship—then hold up your end of the deal! If you want me to cope with all of it, then you don't get to leave all of your stuff there or claim to be an "equal" partner. If you aren't going to help me as I fight to get back on my feet, then how are we equals? You hold all the cards at this moment—if you choose to help a little more over the next six months, I can recoup and take over so that we don't lose the house and you can be happy while we treat the property as a rental investment.

Before this point in our relationship, I had thought that Bill and I had great communication. We had plenty of time to talk, more than most couples. What I didn't take into account was that we never really talked about the hard stuff. In one of our conversations during a family visit, he commented that he thought that committed partners just always overlooked their spouse's faults. I knew from earlier conversations through the years that he would rather walk away from a conflict instead of arguing. I never wanted a big confrontation, but I did want to voice what was bothering me. In my opinion, couples should be able to have a civil conversation about differences and irritants. Overlooking certain faults doesn't have to include not talking about important topics.

When I asked Bill in person or in letters why he loved me, why he liked me, or why he married me, he would never say. He believed that staying with me for twenty-plus years should be enough proof. I didn't need long mushy conversations on a daily basis. Cards and letters were great reminders. He just wasn't good at giving compliments and didn't feel the necessity of telling me what he loved about me. I understood that's not his preferred way to express love, but I wanted to hear it at least once in a while. I knew he loved me in his own way. I heard "I do love you" many times. Was he trying to convince me or himself? I know he enjoyed my company as long as I didn't rock the boat. When asked for a few compliments—even if I was to hear them only once—he couldn't or wouldn't do it. Such a shame.

From his November 15-16 letter:

> I really hope that you get this and stop wanting the same damn questions re-answered when it's not helping anything. How is an answer I give you to this bunch of questions going to solve [the problem] or reassure you? It would be easy to lie about any of them—much easier than the truth—but the fact is that most men don't put much thought into why they fell in love with somebody. Whatever the reasons, when that person starts to accuse them of using her to just pay the bills, when if that were the case there would clearly be a lot of better picks, the warmth and happiness in the bond are not easy to hold on to.

Wow! If he loved me so much, why did he feel that it would be easier to lie to me than tell me his true feelings? Reading that he could have partnered with any of a number of other better women felt like a punch in the stomach. That really hurt. He acted like I should be grateful that he'd chosen me; that he'd lifted me from my pathetic life. It wasn't pathetic at all.

Yes, I kept asking the same questions because not all of our letters reached each other. To make it worse, my letters took longer to reach him (always the case due to the nature of the prison mail system). I used to get all his letters, but not so much when his letters included important family business information. By this time in our relationship, prison staff members were well aware of our marital troubles. Sadly, they would have thrown that in Bill's face.

To make matters worse, Bill never trusted other people easily. I'm not sure where that stemmed from, but he told me about this issue early on in our relationship. That's why we courted each other for five years before marrying. He wanted to be sure he could trust me with his home, his mom, his stuff, and his military information. He also had difficulties taking suggestions from others, even friends, as he felt that he was always right. In his November 17th letter, he wrote that he'd had a call with a long-time friend who spent the time defending me (mind you, he didn't tell me which friend it was). The friend tried to assure Bill that he was misreading what had happened and that I needed his support, not his anger. This friend also told Bill that it's better to try and be more understanding toward those we love and care about, and that it becomes a cold world when we don't trust anyone.

One such trust issue surfaced as we contemplated the logistical problems of how to clean out the house before anyone could start fixing it up to rent. I was not financially able to hire a moving company to take all my stuff to Portland at once. So, I went back and forth several times over the next couple of years to sort, purge, and strategize about what to take, what to donate, and what to throw out. On many occasions, I shipped several boxes of my personal belongings via UPS to my new home. Since that was the most economical way for me to do it, I wasn't keen on Bill asking his friends to come in and pack up his stuff without my involvement, since much of our things needed to be sorted and divided. I didn't want there to be mistakes or confusion about what belonged to whom.

Bill's thoughts on this matter, from his November 17th letter:

> I need to be able to have other people able to come in and remove a lot of my stuff that I want to sell or give away, so we need to work this sort of thing out. You can't come down every time I have people in. My time needs to be spent on things like that rather than lists of emotional drama. I need to fix things that can be fixed, to save what can be saved, not wallow anymore in topics I feel I've already more than covered. I get that you don't want to deal with the house—so let me deal with it! Or work with me on it as a business investment, and not a home. Just please don't put me in this position where I lose it because you want to dump it and don't want to put any time or energy into other options. There are a dozen reasons why I can't lose the house right now—most revolving around any hope I may have about commutation and returning to the community. If we are going to hope for a future together, we need to put together a realistic plan for saving the old place, and for improving our communications on this and other subjects.

Mind you, I was never told about anyone's actual plans to help clear out Bill's stuff. I didn't need to be there physically for that to happen as I could have worked with whomever was to come via the caretaker. He would have been at the house to show them what was what. When I mentioned to Bill that no one showed up even after he'd given me the names of people who were planning to help, he gave me an excuse for why it had never happened—they didn't want to be involved in our divorce drama, and we hadn't even decided to divorce at that point. According to Bill, even his family lost interest in helping fund the house renovation as they thought that if we were splitting up, they would be throwing money at a lost cause after it was fixed up, as I would just take half in a divorce settlement. At that point, they were thinking that the house was somehow community property. I don't really know if Bill's family ever said that. I never met them as they live overseas, I rarely saw their letters to Bill, and obviously, I never heard any of their phone conversations.

Something he wrote on 12-1-20 also meant a lot to me. For a moment, I thought there was hope for us:

> For over twenty years now, I've been a better man with you near me than I was without you, but so much of that was based on our wonderful ability to communicate. As I've told you many times, we have enjoyed a relationship that has been open and likely the first adult bond that has ever lasted in my life. I've thrived on that for years. To suddenly find that on rocky ground has been very hard, and the greatest pain of this very painful year. Believe it or not, the thought of losing you is far more painful to me than that of the loss of the house…and by now you should know how much that means to me.

As I reviewed Bill's letters while writing this book, though, I'm reminded that he took very little responsibility for our relationship woes. He always blamed them on me or on outside influences.

As 2020 was closing, I received a clear example of the narcissist's flare for the dramatic and ability to combine subtle negative messages with loving ones. In his December 23rd letter, Bill wished me a Merry Christmas and hoped I would enjoy the holiday with my family. In the past, I had often visited my daughter before Christmas so as not to leave Bill alone on the holiday, then visited my sister after seeing him. In 2020, that was not to be the case as visiting was still closed due to COVID-19, plus I disliked flying during the holidays. Of course, Bill had to express his true feelings.

> And just so we have one point clear: I'm not happy about you living up there, but I understand it under the current situation and I'm willing to be supportive of it for the moment so that you can be close to your family. Once things have gotten back to normal, we are going to have to have a long talk and see how we can hopefully work things out. For now, be as happy as you can be. Enjoy your family holiday; don't worry about the future because there is no way of knowing what will happen tomorrow. Know that I miss you and sincerely wish we could be together for Christmas.

Little did I know the drama that was yet to unfold.

CHAPTER 5

JANUARY THROUGH EARLY APRIL, 2021

Throughout our marriage, I was sure that Bill had bequeathed the house to me in his will. If that had been the case, I would have sold it to help pay for my retirement after his passing. Bill told me many times that his children did not like America and were not interested in the house. They all had their own fine homes. I didn't marry him just to get my hands on his house or money. Besides, I never even had any proof of his money, let alone access to it.

Bill's will actually states that I was to be allowed to live in the house until I passed, and then it was to go to one of his sons. Since it had been deeded to Bill's trust before we married, it was never community property. I was sent a copy of his will by the attorney to whom he entrusted it for safekeeping. After thinking for many years that I would inherit it, I was shocked and most unhappy to discover that I had remembered incorrectly.

* * *

In his letter dated January 11-12, 2021, Bill told me that he was putting together a list of suggested pathways regarding the house. Again, he emphasized that I needed to remove my stuff from the house "so that I can move forward with what I need to do to either push a caretaker/EDH Center, rent it, or surrender to repairs and sell it. I can't move forward on any front as long as you don't want people in there because of your stuff!"

As long as I was paying for two households, I felt that I couldn't afford to move all my stuff in one trip. It also took time for me to go through my stuff to decide what I wanted to keep. Each time I went to the house to do another round of sorting, purging, packing, and shipping took its emotional and physical toll on me. Besides, there was no firm plan at that point, so what was the rush?

Bill hoped that friends would move into the house for low rent, but that never panned out. I couldn't imagine his friends being willing to put up with "a few problems," as Bill saw it. We discussed the possibility of finding a contractor or handyman who would live there for low rent while fixing it up. That didn't work out, either. He also hoped to eliminate the storage bill by moving things from the storage unit back to the garage. Unfortunately, there were more items in storage than would fit in the small garage.

In Bill's letter of January 25th, he said that it would "take me another year at least—more likely two—before I can take over all of the costs. Yes, I'm stalling a bit—because of the pandemic, I do not have the flexibility I would normally have."

As a narcissist, he was good at making it sound like I didn't try to help ease the stress of the situation at that point, and as if I hadn't been working with him all those years. "If you would work with me on all of this, I believe we can reorganize this year…you need to work with me so we can both come away with something."

So, I suggested that we brainstorm ideas about the house cleanup and creative projects so that we could find common ground in an effort to repair our marriage.

By his January 31ˢᵗ letter, he was clearly unhappy and feeling unsupported on numerous fronts. His friends at the prison were quarantined for COVID-19. He saw my letters as lectures about things he wasn't doing correctly. Remember, a narcissist does not like to be told that he's done anything wrong. "Clearly, we have a very serious breakdown in the peaceful and non-antagonistic exchange of ideas and thoughts right now. So, while I carefully script what I want to say next, let me wish you a happy and healthy February, and a warm and safe Valentine's Day."

In early February, Mark and many of the men in his building were moved to "COVID housing," with an open dorm layout like you'd find at summer camp or a military barracks. Such a setting was not a positive environment and provided no privacy at all. Plus, we were both confused and upset over the inability to really talk the situation through in person. Most of our communications were still by letter only, with a rare phone call now and then. The entire situation was like being on a scary roller coaster.

On top of all that, Bill and I thought that we could add new trustees to his trust. He thought of several close friends he wanted appointed as trustees. Although Bill had written that the house was not more important than our marriage, his letters sounded just the opposite. From his letter dated February 8-9:

> Once the trust is firmed up, then we can talk about the next move, and how to make the property work better for us. For one thing, I'm not pouring half a million dollars into the place to bring its value back up without a written understanding that the trust is set up to protect and serve my interests, and that in the end everyone

understands and agrees that it was always my property, and that the trust is a "friendly gentleman's agreement that will honor my position as the original founder."

Bill also hoped to have a new set of by-laws created to protect his interests: "This doesn't affect your percentage as my wife—all that stays in place—I've got no problem with that. I just have no intention of paying for everything and then having some sort of hostile takeover bump me out of my rightful place." The funny thing is that no percentage was due to me regarding the house. As I said, it was never community property. I never thought of the house as a percentage, but Bill's letter reminded me that everything in our relationship was a transaction—very unsettling.

In the process of researching solutions for funding the house expenses, I had my estate planning attorney review the trust. She pointed out that Bill's trust was irrevocable and couldn't be changed. We couldn't add new trustees. We had thought of asking Barbara, the other trustee and long-time friend of Bill's family, to resign, but decided against it in light of what we'd learned about the trust. Barbara and I hadn't spoken for years, but once we reconnected later in 2021, she became involved in the management of the trust.

Bill and some of his friends thought that a lot of our problems were based on my paranoia about the future, compounded by the stress of the COVID-19 pandemic. From his February 10th letter:

> Your paranoia has grown as misunderstandings and lack of standard communication between us have introduced mistrust, frustration, and anger into the relationship that we had never suffered in the past. Neither of us has

responded well to these negative concepts because we were simply not ready for such feelings—and when we couldn't communicate openly and directly about such questions, the problems expanded.

It is my intention to support you for the rest of your life, without the need to sell our property, and yes, I do have that ability. Yes, I love you—but also I care about you—and I would never leave you for younger babes or rich girls who would bring me more money or political power (I have more than enough of that all on my own—and I don't have the time left to spend on romantic involvements with other women!) So: STOP TWEAKING! Take a deep breath! Relax!

Believe me, you have left me as stressed out about the future as you have been feeling. So, we both need to take a breath, and recommit our hearts and minds to this relationship—because we really are so much stronger when we work together. I do realize that I have not helped this situation. What I'm saying is, let's both stand up and rebuild our respect and care about our mate's outlooks so we can save this union and drop the paranoid thoughts! Neither of us needs any more lectures on selfish expectations or what "we want." We need to rebuild our thoughts to where we were a few years ago when we could overlook the little things to love the good stuff. And put aside the questions when we already know the answers!

I was appalled that he would try to placate me by telling me to just relax. I did not want to be told how to feel and when to calm down. My questions still hadn't been answered. In truth, it was only after the pandemic halted the in-person visits that I awoke to the fact that I'd been lulled into believing that everything was fine. If I listened to his fascinating stories and infinite wisdom on all topics, our life seemed great. In his mind, we could just go back to the way things were in the first twenty years if we could blame our problems on the pandemic.

It was around this time that I realized Bill saw our relationship as lovely, fun, and communicative if I didn't push, question, or make waves. This was compounded by the stress of the pandemic after in-person visits were suspended, and especially after I moved closer to my family. If I visited Bill regularly and went along with most of what he wanted—at least in theory, as I clearly didn't accomplish all of his goals for him—I was under his spell. We seemed to have the perfect marriage. But once I started thinking more for myself and speaking my mind in my letters, Bill would respond with statements like I mentioned earlier: "Clearly we have a very serious breakdown in the peaceful and non-antagonistic exchange of ideas and thoughts right now."

In his February 17th letter, Bill wrote that he was liquidating assets as quickly as he could, but that it might not happen fast enough to pay any of the bills that year. I'd been told that he had numerous items in storage outside of the United States. He supposedly had a stock portfolio and valuable cars. As time went on, it became more difficult to believe in the existence of such things as I never saw any proof and I never saw any proceeds from sales. It was frustrating to think that Bill had resources and hadn't used them to share the burden of the house expenses. Until I was truly anxious about retirement, I didn't realize how I'd let the situation get out of hand and should have brought up the issue of funding the house sooner.

> Thinking we were going to spend our lives at the house when I got out, I never thought that you wouldn't want to help keep it viable until I could take over the full burden. That was my bad, sorry. I should have sold stuff off a long time ago to cover more of the costs of operation. I didn't, because I would have lost a lot of money because that's what happens when you are forced to sell something that isn't in good condition. The same will be true with the house. If you force me to sell it before I get the chance to fix it up and bring it back to its former glory, we'll lose our shirts on it. From your point of view—to get everything you can out of the situation so you can retire and live well in Portland for the rest of your life—it is really short-sighted to slice your nest egg in half (or worse) just to get out from what you see as a burden, instantly. I don't know if it will take me six months or a couple of years to do repairs and clean up the property. When I'm trying to do all this from prison, it's not easy.

I thought that my spending over $100,000 on big property-related expenses—in addition to the normal monthly expenses—was more than doing my share to help keep the house viable. Instead, Bill always had a way of making me look like the wrongdoer for not wanting to continue paying for everything.

In his March 19-21 letter, Bill shared his thoughts about various possible people to use as estate managers/caretakers: prison friends who expected to be released, a contractor who'd be willing to live there for low rent while working on the house, or some of his grandchildren in four to five years. "Once I get my own funds liquidated again, it would be my intention to hire a professional estate manager to handle those funds and everything to do with the house. Whatever still needs to be done around the house to upgrade it, they can oversee."

Whenever I told Bill about the expected costs to do the basic repairs and make the house livable, he would balk. He was sure that his friends could do the tasks for much less money. Plus, he planned to redo everything in several years, when he got out. However, in his March 24th letter, he seemed to realize that the chances of his release might never happen. "I realize that most of my hopes for the future, including my happy return to my home, are likely pretty thin. To that end, there are a number of changes and "surrenders" I will be ready to go along with that I would never have gone with a year ago." He proceeded to provide a list of the household items he absolutely wanted to keep. He unrealistically thought that the items in storage could be moved back to the garage. He hoped that once the basement was cleared out, many of his precious items could be stored there.

His most urgent concern was for his paperwork—legal paperwork for his case and the thousands of pages of creative writing he'd done over the years. He didn't want me to have any of it. He said it should be shipped to his kids, but that never happened.

In his March 27-28 letter, Bill wrote that he had a solution, thanks to certain family members who were trying to help. His children knew a family who was willing and able to do repair work, pay some rent, and help with my nonprofit. We needed to discuss it first, but that never happened, and I never heard from the "lovely family."

At the same time, I thought I had found someone who could act as an estate manager, live at the house, and help with the repairs. He was one of my clients and a professional estate manager. That thought raised our hopes, but that option did not work out, either. Bill clearly didn't trust me to handle these types of arrangements on my own as he thought it necessary to raise numerous questions as if we hadn't discussed them before—was he willing to pay rent, do a little work, handle the daily management?

In his March 29th letter: "So far what I'm being told about the friend is all a bit vague, but I realize it's early days, and I'm more than willing to listen. Now, I've put my people on hold so I can hear out your plan." I hadn't asked him to put his people on hold, and his information about them was much more vague than the information I provided about my person.

It always irritated me that Bill made it sound like I only worked a few hours a day and played the rest of the time. I worked long hours to keep up with my client load (my choice, I know). No, I didn't have people living in my personal space—just three cats— and I didn't have a lot of outside activities, but I was busy. Even though it was his house, he seemed overstretched to suddenly have to think about the house logistics. Also from the March 29th letter: "I'm not sure you realized how much time I'm putting into all of this—or how little time I have for such things. When I have to work eight hours every day, that doesn't allow me a lot of time to write or do anything else. So, you might try to be a little bit more understanding, as I try to find ways to cover all the bills from prison."

Looking back, I find it amusing that, besides thinking of people who could live in the family home, Bill kept coming up with ideas for expanding our income sources so that I could retire "in the next three to five years." I planned to retire, or at least semi-retire, by the time I turned seventy in July 2024. He was hopeful of leaving prison by the time he was 72, which would be in 2025. Then it would take him a few weeks or years to pull together his existing nest eggs.

In his letter dated 4-5-21, Bill suggested that I add new members to my nonprofit's Board and market his numerous books (most of which were, and still are, in manuscript form) and his art and video games (none of which have yet been created). Again, these were all his creative projects—even the nonprofit was largely based on his ideas and information.

In my opinion, he didn't fully understand that obtaining grant funds was not as easy as it was when he was free and obtaining funding for his creative projects. I learned firsthand from publishing my first book that self-publishing is not a quick process and marketing is not always easy. There is a learning curve and much time is needed for research and implementation. The same applies to grant research and applications. Some of the people that Bill suggested I add to the Board were not available. Others were not interested.

CHAPTER 6

APRIL THROUGH DECEMBER, 2021

As I said earlier, we tried to repair the relationship after I moved. Even so, it was like being on a seesaw, or being a yo-yo. One time, my daughter asked me why I stayed with Bill for so long. What kept me in the relationship? I had been so accustomed to the routine—work, weekly visits with Bill, occasional visits with my family, speaking on Bill's behalf at conferences, doing yard work, paying bills, etc.—that I honestly hadn't known the relationship could have been better. I believed Bill when he talked about his past activities, his children, his wealth, and his desire for us to have a wonderful future. I loved his ideas for future romantic dates. He acted like he was a big man on campus and that all the inmates adored and respected him. He was a prolific writer, but that doesn't mean he was writing bestsellers like he was letting on. It was heartbreaking for me to realize just how much he had lied to me.

For twenty-plus years, we followed his agenda for the most part. After I moved and started expressing my opinions more assertively, he made it seem like I was saying that things would only work for us if we now followed my agenda. A narcissist certainly loves twisting the words of the other person. According to Bill, I was reducing his hopes and desires to something to ignore or attack.

It stunned me to see that in just a few paragraphs he would go from expressing positive emotions and feelings for me to making it all about him. He seemingly understood my stress and frustrations but always reminded me of the existence of additional stressors in his life. One minute he was fine with my move and understood the reasons. Then, he'd go right back to hoping we could protect his family home. His bouncing back and forth between kindness and rudeness made it difficult to know whether I was in his favor or not.

An additional frustration was Bill's possessive nature. I was always forthcoming about my daily actions and what I was doing while apart from him, yet that did not work both ways. He kept much to himself. On Easter Sunday, April 4th, Bill called me while I was at my daughter's house enjoying our Easter activities of baskets and brunch. Since my hearing wasn't what it used to be, I moved into the kitchen so I could hear him. In his next letter, Bill wrote that it "felt like you were trying to hide who was calling from everyone else…or 'someone else.'" He was paranoid and distrustful, as if I was cheating on him—something that never happened.

At times I had the audacity to suggest to Bill that he was not always right in his ideas or his agenda. He hated hearing that. In his letter dated 4-8-21, he wrote:

> You are wrong about my intentions; wrong about my design of wording; and wrong about the direction you seem to be heading. I'll leave it at that for now—with the suggestion that you consider what you are doing a bit more. I'm perfectly willing to try and appease your desires and demands (and yes, the word "demands" is correct considering your words and undertone of

implied threat) to a point. But I'm not going to let you insult me or walk on me. That's no way to have a loving relationship or a partnership…and what seems to be a growing lack of respect on your part for who you know me to be, and for my feelings, is not helping. Listening to your words of how kind you've been to allow me an extra few months to rewrite the lost plan to try and propose a way for me to take over all of the overhead and care for the property has me pushed about as close to a place I don't want to go as I've been in years. You want me to "rethink" what I'm writing? Don't worry, I'm rethinking a lot right now. And I would suggest we both do some serious thinking.

April 11: "I do hope our mutual wounds can heal in time. After yesterday's conversation, I believe we are on the same track, although we are going to have to have a number of serious conversations about what 'partnership' means, and the concept of 'working together' to solve problems."

I often felt like a child again, being scolded by my father.

May 16: "Thank you for our nice computer call yesterday. Here's to the rebuilding of a working relationship, trust, and a lasting emotional bond."

In his May 23rd letter, Bill wrote, "My friend's sister is ready to drive down and start packing stuff whenever we tell her." That never happened, of course. When I asked Bill why, he said it was because she didn't want to be involved with our divorce drama, even though we hadn't yet decided to end our marriage. In his May 26th letter, he commented that "our frequent visits had given me a lot of emotional support that made standing up against all the stress and tests that come at me much easier."

Another of my problems was that I was naïve enough to think Bill would be willing to sell some of his assets, like nice cars or some stocks. But it became increasingly clear that Bill did not easily part with his stuff. In his May 26th letter, he informed me that he'd spoken with one of his daughters about auctioning one or two of his antique cars. As I didn't have any concrete information about the car auction plan or knowledge of how such things worked, I kept asking him about it.

In his June 21st letter he said, "Always know how important you are in my life, and that I sincerely do look forward to your communications."

That spring, my book *Midlife Magic* was published. Initially, Bill was happy for me. In his July 4th letter, he said: "Very interesting, and nicely written. Reads well, with an easy flow and good pace. I have no complaints. I am very impressed and very proud of your little work of art."

July 26th was our 19th wedding anniversary and my 67th birthday. His July 22nd card offered "a sincere wish for your continued happiness, and for a hope that we might find a path that works for both of us without parting ways. As we come to the anniversary as well as your birthday, I would hope that both of us might think about being willing to bend a bit to help what has been a rewarding relationship survive."

On September 16th I wrote an angry letter full of my thoughts and frustrations about our situation. I was crabby about the lack of progress or solutions to our house and relationship issues. His October 2nd response letter was angry as well. "So be warned" was written in a box under the date—very dramatic.

I questioned the delay in selling his cars, thinking they would have been auctioned much sooner. "I've told you all along we were aimed at a Christmas-season auction." But I have no recollection of being told that in any of our communications.

I complained about how long it was taking to send me money to help with a roof repair.

> We were locked in the building for a month here and are still in a state of no-program semi-lockdown. There is no way for me to walk into a counselor's office without an appointment. They frown on us sending out large hunks of money to anyone as it looks like we are up to no good—or we are being taken for a ride by a greedy woman.

Also in his October 2nd letter, he wrote that George, one of his inmate friends whom I knew, was granted parole. Bill had hoped that George would get released, live at the house, and fix it up for us. He told me that George's parole would start by the end of the year and that he'd eventually be available on weekends to start cleaning up the old house, selling and packing Bill's stuff, and starting the remodel. George has carpentry skills, so he seemed a natural fit to work at the house. He also has a good business mind and Bill hoped that George would market some of Bill's writing projects. Bill thought that would give him time to organize his funding plan in more detail so that by the spring or early summer of 2022, I could stop paying the house bills. Of course, he had to remind me that COVID-19 had slowed down the whole world, "and then there is the issue that not many men are faced with a wife who wants nothing to do with a family home (except to sell it off)."

Another of our issues was my weight. Bill is about six feet tall, thin, and maintains a regular exercise routine. He has problems with blood pressure and other issues due to his military activities that can't be solved by losing weight and could have easily curtailed our long life together. I have never been petite in my life, but I've not always been overweight. Yes, I overeat or eat poorly when I'm stressed and unhappy. And yes, for much of our marriage, I was overweight. Do some of my current health issues remain a problem when I carry excess weight? Yes. Did I have a regular exercise routine while we were married? No. Several of my previous husbands had criticized me about my weight and withheld physical intimacy at times. It was a very sensitive issue for me.

Did I want to discuss my weight with Bill? No. Did I want articles and tips on taking better care of myself? No. But did I want him to notice and praise me when I worked at losing weight and getting in shape? Yes. And did I want romantic attention from him despite my being overweight? Yes.

I had commented in one of my September letters that Bill hadn't noticed or praised me for my health or weight loss efforts at that time. In his October 2nd letter, his excuse was that in the past I'd told him to "watch it" when he'd wanted to discuss it. He'd given up on saying anything, as he'd hoped that I'd realize that most of my health problems are weight-related and that I would be much better off if I "cut back a bit." He was sure that we would not have a future together (at least one that he wanted) if I didn't take better care of myself. He went on to say in that letter, "I swear, every time I've said something nice in the last ten years, you've turned around and gained weight again. So, don't lash out at me suggesting that I'm not giving you enough positive reinforcement."

There's a big difference between discussing one's weight and receiving praise for one's weight loss efforts. Bill couldn't understand that I didn't need to hear more reasons for keeping the weight off. I had a doctor for that. I needed praise for my efforts in doing so, and I needed to be loved unconditionally when I was overweight.

Bill never found it easy or desirable to discuss hard stuff. His family, his job, and his activities were always a higher priority. So, when I wrote that mid-September letter and spoke my mind, he accused me of pulling a passive-aggressive routine on him in his October 2nd letter. He continued by saying that he did not deserve that! Everyone was stressed by the pandemic. "If I did something to bring this attack on, tell me. I'll try to fix it. But things have become too one-sided in this relationship—with you overlooking everything that I've done that has been positive or for you/us and seeming to admit only what you have done, never admitting to your own mistakes or shortcomings. Well, I can't keep doing a relationship on those levels."

I guess I should be grateful that Bill didn't cuss me out at that moment. Instead, in the October 2nd letter, he reminded me that he was "holding back" on how much he could really say about what I had or hadn't done. He'd put up with a lot, too, and that wasn't easy for him. He had done it for the sake of the relationship. He asked me what options I was offering. In his mind he saw those options as me refusing to help save his home, to sell the house and keep the cash, to stay where I was, and maybe see him once or twice a year if he paid for my travel expenses (I never said that I expected that). In his mind, it was all about me getting my way "without thinking clearly about what taking that path is going to cost you." Reading all that made me feel like I was a disobedient student sitting in the principal's office (something that had never happened to me). I was made to feel like all my decisions to leave and stand up to him were wrong. In his mind, if I just worked with him, I'd be treated with love, kindness, and respect—like a beloved pet. I didn't want to be seen as anyone's pet.

In the October 2nd letter, Bill wrote that his lawyers suggested that I put together a list of what I'd spent on the house so that I could be repaid. No sooner was that penned than he said, "This wouldn't be necessary, of course, if you would relax on the subject and stop making this a 'yours versus mine' relationship rather than a union." He went on to tell me that because I'd been researching options (like selling the house as the trustee) with my attorney, that action was perceived as a threat to Bill and his family.

> This relationship was never about money for me. I loved you and thought that you loved me (not whatever money you might get out of it someday). As a union, I never thought you would get unhappy about helping with the house bills when you were living there. I never

understood how rundown it had gotten, or how unhappy you were there.

I couldn't believe that he didn't realize how rundown the house was. I told Bill how much each repair cost as they happened over the years. It was irritating to see that he conveniently seemed to forget that as if what I wrote in my daily letters didn't matter. I spent over $100,000 on taxes, insurance, fallen trees, and major repairs, yet he made it sound like I was complaining about minor repairs and utility bills. Not to mention that I paid off the bulk of the balance on a line of credit that was outstanding upon his mom's death. In that October 2nd letter, he hoped that I would help him get past the "hard few months" ahead while we waited for George's parole and the funding from the car sale.

At the end of November 2021, we had a family visit. We made an effort to get along and were able to relax a bit for a couple of days. We talked through some issues, but nothing was really resolved. There were no firm plans about the house or news about the car sale. We agreed to keep trying to save the marriage.

By mid-December, Bill was finally able to send the $500 promised months before to help pay for a roof repair at the house. He reminded me in his December 16th letter that I was loved and that he "thought about me around the clock." Even though he expressed good wishes for a happy holiday season, the positive mood was broken when he wrote that he was "working hard to fulfill all of your current requests and desires (and needs and demands)." Reading that took away any joy that he'd originally intended.

CHAPTER 7

JANUARY THROUGH AUGUST 24, 2022

January 2022 arrived. No cars were sold at a Christmas auction as hoped, and I learned later that the auction had been delayed due to the pandemic. While we had hoped that George would have been paroled by the end of 2021, that didn't happen, either. In Bill's January 11th letter, he said that George's parole date was not yet set. Bill assured me that he'd been writing romantic letters, but I didn't get them. We were due to have another family visit on January 31st, but that didn't happen as the number of COVID cases at the prison had significantly increased since our November visit. So many delays on numerous fronts.

In his letter dated January 28-29, Bill wrote, "George and I hope to get the family on the phone this weekend, so we know what is happening with the car project before he leaves." He and George talked for hours about the plans for the house and the creative projects that he wanted George to work on when he was released on parole.

> We have lists, photos, and notes about what he can do or look for as he moves around the old place. Once I can feel more relaxed, with the car funds in the bank, and I know I can cover all the house and property bills for the next ten years, then we can both relax a bit and really take a look at what we want to do with the old place.

Bill's logic was to have George clear out debris, organize stuff, and clean out the basement. He believed that fixing the major sewer problem was easy, affordable, and that George could do it. "I think this is all pretty realistic and shouldn't cause you any stress or outlay. And by the end of the project, we'll end up with our home a finished showplace for us to move into together."

The January 28-29 letter also discussed the new plan for the cars to be auctioned in the spring, provided that COVID-19 was over. The proceeds would be used to open an account for fixing up the house and paying the bills. At that point, I was told that I'd finally have the opportunity to meet one of his family members.

Bill's letters in early February assured me that he missed me and was thinking about me. He wished we could be somewhere on a romantic trip. For Valentine's Day, I wrote him a letter that included a list of the reasons why I loved him. He appreciated it and said that the warm and kind reminder was a large example of the reason that he'd been attracted to me many years ago. A couple of weeks later, we had a nice, relaxing two-day family visit. Bill tried to be more attentive as he must have sensed that his lack of attention was becoming a major irritant for me. No resolutions about the hard stuff, but it was nice to have a break from our drama and relationship woes for a moment.

March 13th letter: "Thank you again for the nice, relaxed family visit. It really proved to be very positive, and the 48 hours meant a great deal to me."

March 23rd letter: "I really do miss you—our 48-hour family visits become huge and vital moments for me, as I hope they are for you as well."

In his May 30th letter, Bill said:

> You know I appreciate your support and continued assistance with things like tax and insurance, and that I'd hoped to be able to step in to take over such payments a half-year ago. Things didn't work out. I'm not going to keep apologizing for things that have proven to be out of my control in this messed-up pandemic era! Shit has happened—and likely will continue to happen—no matter how well I try to get things organized. I'm doing the best I can to get things set up so you can retire and live well in a few years (without being forced to sell my family home)—even if I'm not in your picture. I know I owe you that much. So, please continue to work with me on this, and maybe we can get past these tight and hard times to a point where I'm free and we can both be happy!

May turned into June. Bill had a painful hernia for which he was awaiting surgery. George had not been released on parole. I received no news about the cars being sold. Russia had been at war with Ukraine since its invasion on February 24. I was still working long hours. None of the house or relationship issues had been resolved. I continued to pay for the house expenses.

Bill liked to blame my fears and paranoia on the pandemic as well as on an online journalist who harassed us for several years about Bill's military career and legal case. This journalist went to great lengths to research my past marriages and announced that I'd married several veterans just to get their pensions. He was also convinced that I was staying married to Bill so I could inherit the house. In his mind, I was clearly the gold-digger that Bill's family said I was. He also acted concerned about me as he was sure that Bill was emotionally abusing me. This journalist spoke on podcasts about it. He was producing a documentary about it. Most of the time, Bill wanted me to have no contact with the journalist.

By June 2023, the nasty journalist was still cyberbullying us and had ramped up his attacks on me. Bill's legal team suggested that I start my own podcast to tell our side of the story. Mostly Bill's side of the story, of course. I was not inclined at that point to take on such a project. I love being a guest on podcasts, but they are a lot of work to produce and promote.

The legal team also suggested that I contact law enforcement to complain about the cyberbullying. I did so, but to no avail. The journalist had not physically threatened me and there were no cybercrime units in his area. The local police chief was sympathetic, but there was nothing he could do.

July 2022 was my birthday/our anniversary month, and he wanted to make it a good one for me. We were both quite stressed about our situation. I had not yet received any confirmation of the car sale.

Bill's July 6th letter said, "I realize that both of us are under a lot of stress currently, and that there seem to be a lot of people working against us. I still believe we can overcome these problems and move on with our dreams and happier life if we remember our faith in each other." My faith was waning at that point.

Sometime after the legal suggestions in June about countering the actions of the journalist, I said some things to the journalist in

Bill's defense and mentioned Bill having a health issue. Bill was livid that I had said anything, let alone something about his health. He certainly did not want to appear weak to his enemy.

> Why would you talk to him at all? I've begged you a dozen times to ignore this ignoramus! Every time you try to "help" by correcting him, you are helping him move away from his mistakes to zero in on points that he can twist up to attack me with! There are legal reasons I'm not sparring with this punk. I've told you that in the past. But, who listens to me?

> And the new thrust that I abuse you is a real capper for all of it, because now if I react in any way to anything you do that bothers me, I'm the bad guy and simply confirm what he is saying about me. If you think you are being abused in any way, shape, or form, then leave me! When I think how many times I've bent or stayed silent, just to keep the peace or make you happy, it really ticks me off that I'm the one who gets accused of being the abuser. People may have a fight; that's not abuse!

> He's got you so battered that you've backed away from your podcasts and everything else to do with any message and our relationship is floundering on the rocks. The enemy camp must be roaring with laughter.

Once again, I was made to feel very small and the cause of all our problems. One can only take that for so long.

I continued to ask about the car sale and asked for contact information for his legal team. Bill twisted that around by saying that was "a sad sign of a sudden massive loss of trust and faith on your part. The timing is also odd: just as I'm about to get George out there to get things under control with the house and business efforts." He was not used to me questioning anything after 20 years of blindly believing everything that he said.

Once again, Bill felt he should control the flow of information to me. When I tried to assert myself, he sent this demeaning July 10th letter:

> Let me remind you that I'm not the one who moved away, thus cutting off our ability to carry on a contact relationship on weekends; nor am I the one who has chosen to leave a perfectly savable home for a rented apartment. I understand your reasons, so I've tried to be nice about all of it. Don't get snippy with me now because it takes me a few weeks to organize answers to all your new demands!
>
> If the journalist's crap has gotten to you—I get that, too. But remember, I've never once questioned you about his accusations concerning you, not even now when, quite frankly, you are sounding more like his "black widow," zeroing in to take whatever I have left, than a loving wife worried about her husband who is suffering with a serious medical problem in a careless prison environment.
>
> Yes, we do need to talk about this relationship. It's going to be a two-way conversation, because I'm as tired of a lot of points as you apparently are. If this is all concerning your growing paranoid worry about age and retirement—then get over it! I've got no problem

supporting both of us in the years to come, except when you start questioning me and informing me that I owe you for dental work. I don't owe you for that or anything else! Yes, I know you've gone through a lot because of our union, but your eyes weren't closed when you agreed to be with me. This current "where's the money" and "prove what's out there" push is an ugly and threatening side that I never expected to see, at least not in the woman I took to be my wife.

That letter also mentioned the sale of the car and that it would take weeks to send me proof of the sale. He also mentioned that one of his sons had gone missing in Ukraine, where he'd been fighting against the Russians. That was sad news indeed.

I knew better than to poke the bear, but I did so because I felt justified in asking for information. At that point, it was almost three years since I'd said we needed to have a plan for the house and our future. In addition to my letters, I was also "texting" him through the tablet system provided by the prison. So, he got my questions and comments faster than he did when I just wrote letters. His critical reply on July 11th:

> Try to think out what you are asking me to do before you go off on another insulting tangent about why you don't understand why it takes so long. My question is, "Why do you want or need such paperwork," when you don't have to do anything but sit back and watch as all the bills for the house from here on get paid by me again? Talk about "trust issues." Believe me, right now I've got them, too!

His 7-13-22 card said:

> Perhaps I'm kicking dead hopes at this point—but I'll keep trying for a while. It's hard to give up on a 25-year relationship, even if it seems you've had enough. Time will tell. For now, all I can do is try to make you as happy as I can, considering how we both apparently feel. I'm hurt and tired of all the accusations spoken and unspoken. Maybe we can pull back a bit and try to rebuild things.

In his July 20th letter, Bill told me that the car had indeed been sold, his family had the money, and he'd asked them to send me copies of the contracts so that I could see them for myself.

At some point, I was told that it was a private sale versus a public auction as planned. I never saw any proof of the sale, nor the amount netted.

That letter continued with, "Try to relax, have a nice birthday, and remember that the last 20 years can be a foundation for something wonderful, as long as you don't throw them away." How was I supposed to relax when, in his mind, our future was totally dependent on my behavior? What was the point of continuing the marriage if everything was my fault and he saw no need to compromise?

George was finally allowed to leave the prison on July 25, the day before my birthday. I'd known George for years by that point. Bill and I both had great confidence in his loyal friendship and abilities to help with the house and creative projects.

In his July 25th birthday card to me, Bill said that he wished he was with me so that he could take me to the shops and for some nice meals. That would have been fun, although I'm not big on shopping most of the time. In the sweet anniversary card dated July 28, he said that the garden on the front of the card brought thoughts of the life we'd never enjoyed, and that he felt bad that he'd not been home to enjoy the simple pleasures of gardening, listening to birds, and watching the butterflies together. As nice as that was to read, what I really wanted was to be told how much he valued me as a person. I wanted to know why he liked me other than that I was kind and warm. I wanted to be thought of as an equal. I wanted to feel cherished and loved unconditionally. Was that too much to ask?

On July 31st, he received my letter in which I once again tried to express what I needed from him. Although he sounded like he wanted to work on it, it became clear that my request was not going to be easy for him. He wrote:

> "I got your letter expressing all the ways I could treat you better—or more to your liking. Considering the subject, I am inclined to agree with some of your points. I'm not going to argue it or bring up points that one might bring up as to why romantic thought—or even general relationship kindness—has been derailed. I agree with the overall conclusion that I'm not treating you with the care that wives should expect. It's a rather sad truth, and the more I think about it, the more perplexed I become about how to reorganize my outlook, and the things that have pushed me into the mindset that has created this situation. I shall attempt to address this issue within the

shadows of my mind and heart, and with some luck and effort find ways to do better."

In August 2022, Bill lost his son who'd gone missing in the war in Ukraine. Such a loss was devastating. Bill and his family grieved on separate continents and could only console each other via telephone calls. To make things worse, Bill still hadn't had his much-needed hernia surgery, and he was in terrible pain. Despite our problems, I reached out with several kind and supportive letters that he appreciated. I may not have been happy with the man or our marriage, but it was important to put aside our problems for the time being and show compassion to him and his family. Sadly, he didn't call me for additional comfort as he wouldn't allow himself to fall apart, and he would have felt safe enough to do so with me on the other end of a call.

After that, our days as a couple were numbered.

CHAPTER 8

AUGUST 26-28, 2022

I am patient and compassionate. I understood the pain that Bill's family was going through due to the death of his son, Andriy. I could only imagine the intense grief that they were feeling. I wanted to cry with them and hug them. I'd never met any of Bill's children or grandchildren, nor had any form of phone or email contact with them. Sadly, I couldn't offer my sympathies to them directly.

Life still carried on, much like it does when serious illness or death occurs in a family, and my marriage to Bill continued to disintegrate. I knew I was unwisely poking the bear—which is not good at any time, and particularly not good when Bill was grieving. But I was so tired of waiting for answers and solutions that never seemed to come.

By late August 2022, I was cranky, which was clearly evident in my letters to Bill. I still wanted information about how the house bills were to be paid since the car had been sold. I brought up issues about his irrevocable trust, which was very different from the usual revocable trusts that spouses set up. I wanted to discuss the repayment of the money owed to me by his trust. He wanted more recovery time and was clearly ready to snap.

His August 26th letter opened with, "You asked for this letter, so here it is!" Its eight pages were a lecture about the facts as he saw them. It was as difficult to read as it had been to listen to his lecture from years before in the visiting room, as described in a previous chapter. His ability to use words in a precise, targeted manner truly made me feel like the enemy:

> After the letters of a week ago, I thought you had realized that this demanding "grab-it-all" path you have been on for months was a bad plan and had gone back to being the thoughtful and loving wife that I thought you were for so many years. You can imagine my heartbreak when I read this latest text and realized that you are still on the new path of threat and callous pressure. So, OK—you want a rundown of the facts as I see them; let me lay them out for you.

> For months you have pressured me for money and information, making my life even more difficult than the prison norm. I have done everything I could to satisfy and placate your continued demands, only to be further pressured for more and more. I told myself it was just the hardships of COVID and the journalist's insults and tried to roll with each new punch. I tried to protect you from the growing hate that my family feels toward you, and their outlook that your actions of the last two years have convinced them that you are everything that the journalist has suggested, and are now in the final stages of your game plan to take everything you can get your hands on. Why else would you want me to produce evidence of the car sale, when if you worked *with* me the needed funds would be placed in an account you can see? Why fight me on the idea of setting up George as the

estate manager to handle the funds for fixing the house? What is your logic for slowing that process down, unless you really do plan to cut my throat and use your apparent trustee ability to sell my home out from under me before I can find a way to stop you? I'll tell you right now, you do anything like that, and I'll make sure that you legally never enjoy a dime of my money! Just imagine what you'll face in court if you betray me, with all the smut that the journalist has dug up about your past in the hands of my lawyers. At worst, I'm just a poor old nutcase convict. From the way you've behaved over the last few years, you really do look like the cold-hearted black widow he's made you out to be.

You lived in the house for twenty years, never taking care of it, and by all reports ran the place into the ground. Oh, you paid the basic taxes and insurance apparently, but you let the old house get so run down that by 2020, even you were unable to continue living there. So, you used the COVID thing as an excuse to leave our home to fend for itself—whereupon it was looted and fell into really hard times. Tom told me how little it would have taken to fix the place up if you had just been willing to lift a finger to do it. When he tried, you ran him out of the place.

On the contrary, Tom was not willing to take instructions from a woman. He ended up getting his own place for a while, then moving back to our house for a while, then moving out of the area for his work. When he returned, I left him in place as the caretaker so I could move out of state. He got arrested a few months after I left. That's when the house stood empty and was later burglarized. Thankfully, nothing of great value was taken, and I got it all back from the police later.

Leaving our home to fend for itself, you refused to clean it up so we could rent it; refused to work with me to have anyone I know come in to clean it up; and started pouring all your money into rent and publishing your little "book" about your life. When I think what could have been done with any number of my own creative works if you had put half as much time or money into them as you have into that little memoir, I really have to wonder how much money we might have in the bank. Even now, when I try to have George get in there to see what can be done to save the old place, you have tried to block my every move and now brought up the threat that you have such control of the trust that you can sell the place out from under me, no matter what I do.

Knowing how much my family home means to me, most people would have assumed that a real wife might have tried to be a little more willing to take over the long-range ways to save the place. But when I offered to raise all the funds needed to not only fix the place, but to care for it from here on so you never had another bill of any sort concerning its care, you have done everything in your power to slow my efforts, demanded that I prove that I sold my beloved old car, and pushed me on every crazy point you could think of, from addresses of appeal lawyers to sending you $500 to help pay for a roof repair! Your behavior has been nothing less than odd, frequently on the edge of deliberately inducing stress, and altogether unfriendly—not something one would expect from a loving wife.

I made the mistake of trying to appease you, and then trying to be kind to you about the reasons that I could not fulfill your demands. That's my bad. Believe me, it isn't going to happen anymore. I'm fed up with me looking bad because I'm trying to protect your feelings and with me putting up with your nasty rants and accusations for months.

The truth is, I never blocked George from checking out the house. He wasn't able to leave his transitional housing for a few months after he started parole. Bill never put me in touch with any of his contacts who supposedly were going to help clean up the house. Regarding his creative projects, he assumed they would each be largely successful and make lots of money. My book sold more copies than the two fiction books of his that I published. I did not intentionally slow his efforts to raise money. I only wanted concrete information. So, to read his letter continually vilifying me was exhausting and annoying.

At the time, Bill was apparently rewriting his last will and testament to adjust the section relating to what I was to inherit upon his death if we were still married. The original version stated that I would inherit his property and possessions in the county where the house is located, and that I was allowed to live in the house until I died, at which point it would go to his son Jacques. By the time he wrote this letter in August, his feelings on the matter had changed:

As it stands at this moment, I have no intention of signing the rewritten nice version, because you have me so pissed off at this point, and are so paranoid that you are looking for excuses to leave me, that I see no reason why I should give you as much as I had intended. As it stands right now, my kids will fight you for everything that rightfully belonged to me anyway if anything happens to me—just out of spite for the way you've acted over the last two years. Sad, too, because before your COVID wig out, they had actively been talking about finally taking you in as part of the family.

Mind you, I had never heard about the possibility of his children finally accepting me and wanting to meet me until that point.

How many times was I to be subjected to one of his lectures without getting any real answers? I was relieved that I didn't hear these words in person, but I could feel Bill's anger and condescension as if I were sitting next to him in visiting. Once again, he managed to humiliate me and rile me up in ten pages.

It was obvious that Bill no longer trusted me and that my letters were provoking him. Yes, I had told him that, as a trustee, I had the power to sell the house if it was in his best interest. But I had never indicated any interest in taking all the money from such a sale, or taking any of his other precious belongings.

On top of all of this, Bill didn't believe what I'd told him about his irrevocable trust. He'd apparently forgotten he had set up this kind of trust. He was sure that more trustees could be added, but that was not possible. He wanted more checks and balances for the use of the money from the car sale, as he was sure that I'd misspent his inheritance. The money left after his mother passed was spent on things per his instructions—a remodeled room, garden items, a used car for me, and other collectible items that he wanted me to buy. When I worked with the other trustee, I provided a detailed list of how Bill's inheritance was being spent. It was shocking to me that he didn't accept responsibility for telling me how to spend that money. As I've said before, a narcissist doesn't ever think they've made mistakes.

On the other hand, if it was my money that was being spent— especially if it was spent on the house or Bill's projects—Bill didn't complain. Once I started saying that I wanted to be reimbursed for what I'd spent on the house's big expenses, he would try putting me in my place, reminding me that a good wife should not mind helping to pay the household expenses. Such reminders were infuriating as we were not living in the 1950s of our childhoods. I did not want to be thought of or treated like the housewives portrayed in the family TV shows we watched as kids like *Leave it to Beaver* or *The Donna Reed Show*.

I was counseled by an estate planning attorney, who said it was my legal right as trustee to be reimbursed for funding the expenses of the trust's asset (aka the house). I told Bill about these discussions in my letters to him. In his August 26th letter, Bill responded with this: "Some of your points about how you want to be repaid for money you've put into the house really chap my hide. I will pay you whatever you can put forward as your investment, just to end any misunderstanding and cut any further demand you think you have on the property."

Over and over in that letter, Bill emphasized that he had provided his family home for me in a nice neighborhood, that I should be ever-so-grateful, and that it was reasonable for the wife to pay some of the expenses.

As a married couple, with the husband in prison, most people would not consider it too out-of-the-question for you to be expected to cover some of the costs for the house you were living in. If I had ever known that you felt put-upon, I would have sold off most of what was in the house, and whatever else I had left a long time ago and rented the place. Now it's almost too late to do that as you've dumped the whole thing in my lap after your move. Anytime I've tried to get people in there to clean it out, you've made it too complex to do that. So, yes, I'll pay you what you think you put into the house—but consider it a buyout, with you having no legal interest in the property after that. After telling you I was more than ready to cover us both in retirement, I really don't get this whole direction you've taken with recent demands— nor does anyone else—and it doesn't bode well for a positive image.

Reading those words made me feel sick. I felt like I was expected to act like the servant who should be so grateful to have a place to live and work that I wouldn't mind the long hours and difficult tasks I was meant to perform. I reminded Bill more than once that I was probably the only prison wife in that county, and most likely the only one living in one of its nice neighborhoods. It would have been hard enough to live there if both spouses were working, let alone when one must rely on the income of their spouse.

As for Bill covering both of us in retirement, I had also reminded him (again, more than once) that there was no guarantee he would be released and that there was no proof that his assets would cover our retirement. For too long, I had lived on blind faith that Bill had been telling me the truth. So, if he was telling the truth, why was it so hard for him to provide any evidence to back himself up?

Have you ever watched a hamster running in the wheel in his cage or a dog chasing its tail? That's how I felt as I read this August letter. I felt like I was going around in circles, hearing more excuses than answers. Bill's August 28th letter was included with his August 26th letter as he allowed himself a day to reign in some of his anger toward me. In this letter, he wrote, "Yes, I realize there are bills to be paid, and we aren't too sure how to do that at this moment. The money will be there. We are doing what we can."

Bill had clearly counted on George being released from prison a few months before he was. For that reason, he had hoped that systems would be put in place to manage the money from the car sale and pay for remodeling/cleanup expenses. Even though Bill and I had not decided to divorce yet, he was still not considering me as a temporary solution for handling the money for the most immediate needs. If the main source of funds couldn't be arranged, Bill's contingency plan was for George to find certain things in the house that Bill was willing to sell. However, since George had limited time and no choice but to rely on public transportation, this was not a good option for raising money quickly.

In the August 28th letter, Bill asked for a list of all the house-related expenses that would be due within the next six months, which I provided. "That way I can try to put it together either as advances on the main sum, or from other sources." Reading this did not instill confidence in me that the car sale had ever happened.

Finally, thanks to my past experiences with marriages and divorces, I already knew that both parties say things toward the end of the relationship that are unkind and don't need to be said. But with Bill—and, I imagine, with most narcissists—the barbs were venomous, like this last excerpt from his August 28th letter:

> Yes, I *do* grasp that you (and whomever you are talking to) have questions about *if* I'm telling you the truth about incoming funds. Time will tell. Just remember, I now have similar questions concerning whether you've changed from being the loving wife into some sort of example of the "gold-digger" that others have accused you of being. Again, our faith in each other has been shaken—and if we are going to save this relationship, we *both* need to work on it.

By late August 2022, I'd been in therapy for almost two years. I'd learned much about narcissism. In those sessions, I cried; I laughed; I shared how one minute, Bill was loving, and then as soon as I crossed his line, he wasn't. I would explain how he would begin by being understanding, then put all the blame on me in his letters. I could share the full spectrum of my feelings as I worked with her. The more I learned about narcissism, and the more we worked together, the more I saw the patterns. Unless I gave in to Bill every time, it would always be my fault in his eyes. I was worn out, but I was healing and growing at the same time. I was finding new strength to be myself.

CHAPTER 9

SEPTEMBER THROUGH NOVEMBER 1, 2022

This pattern of Bill being understanding one minute and blaming the next showed up again in his September 6-7 letter, when he shared that (according to him) *everyone* he knew was telling him he was a fool to be nice to me and to try to save our marriage:

> What woman who wants to stay in a relationship talks about charging for what she has spent on the home she has lived in for 20 years? Most would be working to keep it up, and help with what that took, so they could count on living there with their husband in the future. Clearly, you aren't counting on that.

His constant digs were meant to wear me down, and I became more offended with each such letter. How was I supposed to run my business, keep up with the house bills and needed repairs, visit Bill regularly, and continue to help with his creative projects—all at the same time? It was all too much to expect of me. For twenty-plus years, I had been working to please him, support him, and love him. But when I finally expressed my concerns and needs, Bill wasn't used to being questioned, not believed, or held accountable for answers from his partner. In his mind, my behavior was unjustified, and all he could see was this angry, demanding woman.

Also from his September 6-7 letter:

> You seem to believe it's all my doing, while I believe to my core it's all your doing. Either way, if we don't work it out soon, I'm going to lose everything. That does not please me, considering how well the legal push is going and that I may be free in a relatively short time. Between COVID and Smith, we've had a rough three years—but I'm not going to be the fall guy for that! So, stop snapping and insulting me, and at least try to be friendly while giving me the facts to get things moving forward and fixed.

Bill sounded like a broken record. All the years I've known him he complained about how others blamed him for everything going wrong in the world. No one had ever blamed him for COVID, or for the trouble we'd had with the journalist, Smith. Rather, it was aggravating that Bill refused to take any responsibility for his part in our failing marriage.

On October 1, 2022, I saw Bill in person for one of the last times. It was not a family visit, so we spent several hours talking in the regular visiting room, within earshot of other inmates and their visitors. Such a setting was not conducive to an important private conversation like ours. Like every other visiting room visit, I was assigned to our seats. I got our snacks. I waited for Bill to enter the visiting room. I was anxious about the upcoming bills due that Fall.

"Bill," I said. "The house insurance bill is due next month. The property tax is due no later than December 10th. How are they to be paid?"

He replied, "I'm not sure yet. It takes longer than you think to get the answers you want. Please remember that the boys who would normally sign checks are all off doing their military duty, while the women still haven't recovered from Andriy's passing, and are in no mood to hear my begging for money for my house. I know the time to cover the payments is getting short. You don't need to remind me every day of everything I need to do. I may be old and sick, but my brain is apparently failing only in your eyes."

It was a tense visit, and nothing was resolved. I was expected to wait, as I'd been doing.

George finally saw the house on October 2nd. I gave him the grand tour, then he walked around and through the house on his own.

"Jo Ann," he said. "I'm quite concerned about all the problems that I see. It really is not salvageable. I see cracks in the foundation. The wooden deck is full of dry rot. The main retaining wall is bowing outward in certain places. There is visual evidence of earth movement on the hillside. There is evidence of rodent and spider activity in the house. There is exposed wiring that needs to be replaced. Plus, I see water damage. I don't think that the house is salvageable. I want to help Bill, but it's more of a project than I want to take on. Plus, I'm not allowed to leave my assigned area for more than six hours at a time for at least a year. That doesn't give me much time to work at the house."

He wrote a long letter dated October 11th to Bill about his findings, only to have Bill say that George was now my big defender.

Bill's October 15th letter reported conversations with his adult children. I'd already sent detailed information to Bill about how to pay the property taxes and insurance online, so he said that "with exact locations to send the funds they saw little reason not to do that." Without George on-site to manage the remodel, though, Bill's family was reluctant to put forth any money. The insurance payment was withdrawn from my account in error, as I'd forgotten that it had been set for automatic payments. This confused Bill's family when they tried to pay the bill. Of course, it was all part of my "evil plot," according to them, and I was never reimbursed. Nor did they pay the property taxes that were due that fall.

George reminded Bill more than once that I'm a bookkeeper. There was no sound reason for me not to be involved in the handling of the car sale proceeds that were to be used for the house remodel and other expenses. I'm excellent at my profession, and I had a fiscal responsibility as one of the trustees to manage the trust's asset—namely, Bill's house. I never intended to steal his money or mismanage any funds provided to remodel the house or pay off the growing debts. If Bill indeed had the money to take care of his house, great. There would have been no need to talk of selling the house.

By the end of October, Bill's family knew about the contents of George's letter. They concluded that the house was not worth saving or throwing money at. No wonder Bill was quite dramatic in his letter dated November 1st:

> So, you've won. I'll put together a basic list of the few
> things I want saved, where to donate some other items if

others want such things, and who might accept a few gifts. I don't know how a lot of this is going to work, and need to talk to George and several others before we firm up any plans, but let's get a better idea about an estate sale, and what sales price is realistic for the property at this point. Couldn't be a worse market, but that is just one more part of the story, and an example of why I'm not going to pretend to be the least bit pleased with the current situation. We might ask the neighbor if he is interested in the property once we have an idea of what the market value is—since he is a big reason that we are leaving. Anyway, a hard, sad day for me. I had never expected to suffer this loss or all of the endings that would go with it. Grandchildren will no longer come to California to go to school. My bloodline will no longer own a holding or a family seat in the county as established by my father in 1949. I'll no longer have a way to store my papers or things and will be forced to change all my plans.

The neighbor whom Bill mentioned owns the driveway that passed the house. Before the Great Depression, the driveway belonged to Bill's house and led to the living room entry on the uphill "back side" of the house. During the Depression, the original lot was subdivided by the owner, and a second house was built at the end of the driveway. Anyway, the current neighbor was often annoying, as he seemed to feel it was okay to suggest to me improvements for Bill's property. Even so, he was not my reason for leaving the area or for wanting to sell the house.

Bill continued his rant from the November 1st letter:

> Without the property to tie me to a family location, a large portion of my argument for a secure parole is removed. I become just another ex-con, without ties to any local community. And the loss of the house, under the present conditions, is going to thrill Smith, as it all but proves his rants about your motives for our relationship.
>
> So, here I sit, watching the apparent crumbling of all my hopes for the future. I realize I can recover with major changes to my plans. It will make it harder for me to get out of prison and will leave me next to nothing to get restarted on my own. But my options are still out there. I have no intention of going into Vet housing. I mentioned that only as my interest in what is offered to others. I'm not a renter or a beggar, but the loss of family possessions will bother me forever, and very likely make me a very bitter old man.

It was disheartening to realize that my hopes for the future never factored into the unfolding scenario. My losses or broken dreams never mattered. It was true that the government considers an inmate's family home as part of the consideration of their parole approval. However, Bill was not willing to buy a smaller property if (or when) it looked like he was close to being released. Yes, he and his family owned some cool things, but they were just things. If his possessions had burned in a fire, he would have needed to adjust. Even though Bill swore to me that I meant more to him than his things, that was clearly never the case. The line in the sand was drawn. His house and stuff were more important than our marriage.

Bill then went on to say this in that letter:

> There is no further reason for you to be stressed out. You've gotten what you want. In a matter of months, you'll be rid of the house and any bills related to me or my needs. You'll likely get out of it with something for yourself, with nothing further to be bothered with. I sincerely hope that makes you happy.

So, there we were. Divorce was inevitable. We could not resolve our differences and were no closer to settling on what to do about the house. Due to my history of failed marriages, I was not keen to add another divorce notch to my belt, but it was more important that I move on and take care of myself.

CHAPTER 10

NAVIGATING THE DIVORCE

Even at the time of Bill's November 1st letter, the word *divorce* was never actually said. We both had just given up and knew that divorce was the next step. Neither of us wanted to say the 'D' word, but that's what we were facing. We were each resigned to that reality. Even in the years leading up to it, going through with a divorce was still painful.

On November 21-22, I had a family visit with Bill. We agreed that it would be a business meeting to discuss the logistics of a divorce and how to clear out and sell the house. Those two days were very uncomfortable. We had a heated discussion about what had gone wrong in our relationship, not that it helped at that point.

"Why didn't you support my book?" I asked once again, hoping his answer might be different since we were discussing it in person.

"The timing wasn't good for my case. It made me look like a loser like your other husbands."

"Why didn't you want to kiss me more and show more affection?" I asked.

"You should have tried to be prettier." Shocked by his callous remark, I started crying and stopped talking to him.

On November 26, Bill wrote me a letter where he claimed that he was busy redesigning his life and future: "No reason to sit around any longer, or to work toward a path that is no longer going to be waiting for my return." Although I thought divorce was the best solution, it still hurt to read how quickly he cut off his feelings for me and I became persona non grata.

Once again, it seemed that he was more remorseful about losing his home and the dream of living forever in the area where he'd spent his youth than he was about losing me. He made it clear that he'd always hoped to revisit his favorite places in the county where he'd grown up. Most of those places were now gone except for the lovely neighborhoods. Just because Bill would not own the house any longer was no reason for him not to visit the area. That made it much easier for me to proceed with the divorce and start to move on with my life.

In December 2022, we explored the possibility of selling the property to the neighbor who owned the driveway. He was interested in doing so, expressing his desire to demolish the house and leave the hillside as open space for the local animals. Unfortunately, he only wanted to pay an amount much below the market value. So, that idea was discarded.

In early February 2023, I left Oregon to go to Bill's house in California with the plan to list it with a realtor. Once there, I worked with an organizer to sort, purge, pack, and donate the belongings left in the house. Going room by room, we made excellent progress in just a few days. We laughed a lot and joked about how much stuff was in the house—three households' worth. I knew which of my smaller household items I wanted to send home to Oregon. I knew basically what Bill wanted to save from his and his parents' things. The rest seemed "fair game" to donate or throw out.

During that time, I was in contact with Barbara, the other trustee, who had agreed that it was best to sell the house. Toward the end of the week, though, she called me at my hotel telling me that she'd received a letter from Bill expressing his sadness about selling the house and how he really didn't want to do so. This was the complete opposite of what Bill had told me in a text message on February 5, when he'd wished me good luck with the packing.

Since this was the first time Barbara and Bill had been able to communicate in years, Barbara wanted to hear him out and understand his wishes. Thus started the process of her finally stepping into her role as an active trustee.

I was livid about the new delay and confronted Bill about it via text. He replied on February 9 and said this:

> I told her the truth. You know I don't want to sell my home. Sadly, I also realize that I'll likely have to. I also need to establish a method for any income to be managed fairly, and for whatever portion that is being provided to me to come to me and remain under my control. I'm never going to be put in this position where my property is controlled by others! So don't get your panties in a bunch. This was the first letter Barbara seems to have gotten in years, and I needed to let her know that I'm not a happy camper with what is being forced on me. That doesn't mean you aren't going to get your way. It just means that I want a few checks and balances to make sure I don't lose everything!

The house was not put on the market then, and all work with the organizer stopped. I shipped home the last of the things I wanted: books, photos, favorite kitchen items, crafts, and framed needlework pieces. That still left lots of household goods to be dealt with: furniture, Bill's creative writing projects, more books, Bill's legal paperwork, and collectible items he'd had me buy over the years.

Over the next several months, I provided information to Barbara about my relationship with Bill and the house expenses—all things that she had no clue about. After all, she hadn't seen him for years and knew very little about his life. Her memories were mostly of his parents. She only had a few of Bill and they were from when she was a young girl. She was quite surprised at most of what I told her. For example, she never knew that he was in the military or that he had any children.

Any messages Bill and I exchanged in late February and March were discussions about family or sentimental items. For example, I wanted to keep my engagement ring. Bill, however, wanted me to return it, as it was also his grandma's ring. Mind you, I had worn it for twenty-plus years by then, and engagement rings are considered gifts from the groom to the bride. Bill had wanted me to leave it in a safe place in his house, though. I decided against that and offered to return it to one of his daughters if she was willing to travel to the US to get it. I was even open to traveling to her if my expenses were covered. But in the end, I kept the ring.

I had also hoped to take—or at least borrow—some family photos and Bill's writings about his father so I could include them in a book I was planning to write. But Bill refused to give me permission to do so.

Then there was the matter of a golden crown Bill had had me commission our jeweler to make. Who knows why he'd wanted it. If nothing else, it was a strange way to invest some of his "inheritance"—aka his mom's money—and his lineage goes back to a German princedom on his dad's side. Hence, the word *prince* in this book's title. Anyway, I had the crown with me for safekeeping and wanted to sell it. Bill didn't want it sold, however. I didn't know his true reason for having the crown beyond using it as a marketing tool for one of his business ideas that was never developed.

In addition, Bill said several times that he would consider paying me a divorce settlement—above what was owed to me for the house expenses—only after the divorce was final. He refused to even discuss amounts until that point. I hadn't expected any type of settlement as I had no proof that he had any real money. If he did, then a settlement seemed only fair. I was hoping to be reimbursed somehow for his half of the divorce fees. I wasn't holding my breath, though.

As we continued to text back and forth about money, photos, the ring, and the crown, Bill still tried to maintain control of the situation. His attempts to do so didn't bother me. What could he really do to hurt me further?

When Bill texted me on February 27, he said this:

> I have to admit that I'm not happy with the direction of some of your recent suggestions. You seem to be under

the misconception that because I've tried to be nice about the situation you can have everything your way. From me paying you ransom money for items that are clearly mine to start with to the thought that you can continue to take anything you want, like family pictures, for you to include in a book about my father (something you will not do with my permission under the current conditions), will be fought out in court if you keep on this path of trying to grab everything. I'm perfectly willing to have a rational conversation about a settlement—and try to keep the effort civil. But your expectations seem to be getting way too crazy at this point for someone who went through my entire inheritance, ruined my home, and enjoyed trips to England rather than perform a little upkeep on a place that at the time was considered "our" future home. Since I am now expected to pay all of the bills for "my" home, I will presume that you are out of the house, so that I can have my people come in and do an inventory, locate what items of value may still be there for the insurance company, and do a full inspection for condition. This has to be done before I continue with any conversation about further asset exchanges or make any final thoughts about what my plans for the property may be. And let me add, you don't give me orders concerning how the only way to get my grandmother's ring back is for my daughter in England to fly over here to personally get it from you. Clearly this is not going to be as easy as I had hoped.

Then, on March 10, in one of his last texts to me, Bill said a few things that surprised me—and a few others that didn't:

> You may not legally have to return Baba's ring. But when it means as much as it does to my family, and nothing to you but the money value, one might think that you would consider it. If I have to purchase it back from you, we can talk about that. Let me point out that you are the one talking about wanting me to sign paperwork. Well, the more you demand from me, the more it comes around. You started your business in my house, putting my needs on the back burner. You sold big items like the safe to pay for your book, putting all of my efforts aside. You think that's all going to be forgotten now, as you charge me for "packing" my things in the house rather than calling George and other supporters and getting it done for free? All of a sudden, I'm getting billed for things that I've never heard of from ten years ago, and you think I'm just going to roll over and pay it all without some question? Barbara knows about future funding—but she also understands that we have bills to be paid now, and I've got nothing until this divorce is final—and that could take months. Barbara is being realistic, and looking out for my best interests. So if you want this to be "easy," then consider what you are demanding, and who you are dealing with. All you need to do is be realistic, too. Let Barbara have the keys to my house so we can get my people in there to start cleaning and checking to make sure everything is still there that should be there, and we'll work out a realistic settlement that we can both agree to.

A lot of this must sound like a case of "he said, she said." That's very sad, when you think about it. To clarify part of what Bill said on March 10, the income from my bookkeeping business paid for the house bills. When I sold the large safe—which Bill had wanted me to buy years before—the money also went toward paying household bills. And since I was the one who was working, I'd figured, why not use some of my own income—not the money from selling the safe—to pay for publishing my first book? But Bill made it sound like I'd never told him about the big house expenses, when in fact I'd written to him about them regularly, telling him what repairs were needed and how much I'd paid for them.

After the March 10th text, Barbara was given the keys to Bill's house. No one contacted her about going there to continue the cleanup.

* * *

Thankfully, getting a divorce in Oregon turned out to be much easier than getting one in California. I didn't know that at first and went around in circles for a few months. First, I contacted a family law attorney in Oregon recommended by my daughter. That lawyer thought I should talk to one who was licensed to practice law in both states and referred me to such an attorney. The second lawyer listened to my details and suggested that Bill and I sort out the house issues and other financial pieces before filing for divorce.

Once I thought Bill and I were making some progress with the logistics, I contacted the second lawyer again. She was too busy at that point, and her assistant suggested that I work with a

California lawyer. The first one I called did not want to take on our case, as Bill lived in another county. The second California lawyer eventually said the same thing. Plus, they both sounded like having spouses in two different states made it more complicated. This all sounded strange to me, but what did I know?

I went back to the drawing board and contacted the first Oregon attorney again. Barrett and Jones Law only handle cases that do not involve litigation, which was fine with me. The retainer was lower than it would be if we anticipated going to court. I worked with an associate rather than one of the partners as her rate was a bit lower than if I had worked directly with one of them.

My new lawyer, Karen Perry, said that we could proceed along the lines that it was a mutual decision and there were no demands on the other party. We agreed that the divorce paperwork would assume that Bill had no assets, since he was incarcerated, and I couldn't prove the existence of such assets. I authorized Karen to set up the paperwork stating that me and Bill would agree to be responsible for our own debts and that there would be no settlement agreement. I also wanted it stipulated that Bill would agree that he was not entitled to half of my retirement fund or my self-employment earnings. Fortunately, my lawyer had prior experience with sending legal paperwork to a prison, which made that part of the divorce proceedings easier for me.

After that, the divorce would likely be a smooth process—unless Bill decided to contest it, of course. Since I wasn't demanding anything, I couldn't imagine what he could possibly contest. I had to be ready for that possibility, though.

I signed the dissolution documents on March 23, 2023. They were filed with the court on March 28, and a case number was assigned on March 31. My attorney's office informed me via email of further details about the process, saying, "We wanted to make you aware that after discussing this case with the firm, and because the work we are doing is based on him signing the documents, we will be sending him a letter to show it's coming from you and not our firm and ask him to return the signed documents to you. The documents were set up so you are your own attorney for the purposes of the court case. We did it this way so that if you need to hire someone in the future for a litigation case, that would be easy to do."

The paperwork was sent to California. Bill was officially served the paperwork by a prison staff member on April 13, 2023.

April 14th was our last in-person visit. I was not looking forward to seeing Bill, but it was easier than I thought as I felt rather detached at that point. Entering the visiting room as usual, I was assigned to sit at a high table which was more comfortable than the low ones, and it would just be the two of us. I got sodas as usual. Bill entered the room, and we hugged as usual.

I told him straight out, "I just want you to know that as of May 1st, I will no longer be paying for the house expenses. I wanted to tell you in person since you don't get all my letters or texts. I don't want there to be any 'I didn't know' from you."

"Fine," he replied. "That won't be a problem. I can handle the smaller expenses."

"I want you to know that I did love you," he claimed.

"Hmmm," was all I could say, as that was too little, too late.

"You were mean to me sometimes in visiting, and you wrote mean letters to me after I left the house," I said sadly.

"I don't remember ever being mean to you," was his reply.

Standing by the door as we said goodbye, I felt detached. Twenty-plus years down the drain. I no longer loved him, and I never wanted to see him again. Bill said, "I'll miss you and I hope we can remain friends.

"We'll see," was my response, but I knew that would not be the case as I walked out of the prison for the last time.

* * *

I received Bill's signed documents on April 24 and rushed to my attorney's office later that day. I was never so excited to pay for a Lyft ride. My stress from this untangling process started to melt away. I was ushered into the conference room at the law firm's office. My attorney wasn't there so I spoke with Amy, assistant to the attorneys.

"Please sign here and here," she said as she presented me with a few final documents. "We will file this paperwork with the court tomorrow. It's just across the street. The last step will be for the judge to sign the final decree. It might only take a couple of weeks."

"That's great," I replied. "The waiting period in California is six months."

Soon after, I was on a cruise with my sister and brother-in-law.

As we enjoyed our evening cocktails, I checked my emails. "Lee, I have an email from my attorney. The divorce became final on May 2, 2023! Woo hoo! It's time for a toast and a happy dance!"

As for a "divorce settlement," Bill had said he would consider one, but not until the divorce was final. During that finalizing process, Barbara kept asking how much I wanted as a settlement. I knew that Bill's trust owed me more than $100,000 and that Bill owed me for half of the cost of obtaining the divorce. There were also other house-related expenses that I paid after my May 1st deadline, such as another tree emergency in April and the removal of flammable weeds in August. I told all of this to Barbara verbally, along with a written list of the expenses paid and copies of the receipts.

Oregon sent each of us a copy of the "Notice of Entry of Judgment" to inform us that the judge had signed the paperwork and that a judgment lien was created for any monetary award stipulated in the divorce. We received our copies of this notice before we received our copies of the final decree. Our final decree clearly stated, "No Money Award." This did not include the money that the trust owed me nor Bill's half of the divorce legal fees. As mentioned earlier, I couldn't prove that Bill had personal liquid assets, so I didn't request a monetary award in the divorce paperwork. Doing so would have caused more problems with Bill and delayed the divorce process.

We began a series of texts to discuss the divorce becoming final and the money piece:

May 13:
Me: Divorce is final...signed by judge on May 2.

May 14:
Bill: Happy Mother's Day.

Me: Thnx. Enjoying the cruise. Will you now move ahead with freeing up your money for the house?

May 15:
Bill: Before I can do anything, I need to have the signed final paperwork proving the legal action is finished.

Me: I have asked the atty to mail you a copy. You can set up your plan while you wait for it.

May 23:
Me: Did you get your copy of the divorce? It was sent by the court.

May 24:
Bill: What I got was a letter from the court informing me you put a lien on my property!

Me: It is a standard part of divorce judgment...in the middle of the page it shows no $$. I did not ask for any money in the divorce as shown in the docs we signed and I did not put a lien on the house. The signed judgment says 'no money award.' I will mail the 1st page and signature page. Hopefully you will soon get your full copy. I got that lien thing before the full copy, too.

June 1:
Bill: No sign of any paperwork, other than the court's info letter informing me about the lien. As long as that lien is in effect, my chances of saving the property, or

getting any sum of value out of it are non-existent. It would be helpful if you removed it.

Me: There is no lien. I did not ask for any money. You know that from the papers you signed. On the back of that paper it clearly states that the judge has signed the final paperwork. I just confirmed with my lawyer that 'no money' shown on form means no lien created. Standard form to show that judgment was signed and entered with court. Barbara has copy of form and lawyer's email and the divorce doc. She can confirm that it is all final.

Regardless of what Bill believed, the judgment and final decree clearly showed that no money or support was awarded to either of us.

CHAPTER 11

MOVING ON

It is now March 2024 as I fine-tune this last chapter before publication.

Despite what Bill wrote in November 2022 about me winning, it was never about winning for me. I never saw our relationship as a competition. Yet, to a certain extent, the drama continues. The divorce has been final for almost a year, and I did stop paying for things, but all issues have not been resolved.

No one has gone to the house to take inventory of the belongings for insurance purposes as Bill said would happen. None of his children or grandchildren have arranged to collect and ship the precious family belongings that he said they wanted. Bill has not introduced Barbara to anyone in his family.

Bill's funding of the house expenses has not materialized. None of the alleged car sale proceeds have been transferred to the trust's bank account, regardless of what he texted to me a year ago. There was never any actual discussion of a divorce settlement beyond me telling Barbara what I am owed by the trust and how much the divorce cost.

March 5, 2023, text:

> My funding of the property needs will take place as soon as the divorce is final. The only hold-up for that will be

some thoughts about the sum you want paid, and how quickly you expect whatever we agree on. As I've said before, I don't mind some sort of settlement, but you need to remember this is a two-way street. It's not going to be all your way.

In a text after Barbara's visit with Bill in August 2023, she told me that she gave him three to six months to see what could be done before putting a hard stop to the waiting and preparing to sell the house. She quickly learned that the situation was complicated—and that it wasn't easy working with Bill. There was no mention of him having any money. He still thought I had a lien against the house.

I've worked with Barbara to save Bill's house from foreclosure and buy more time before selling it, as that seems to be the inevitable and most logical outcome. Bill has other plans, of course. He told Barbara that he wants to donate it to a nonprofit group that helps formerly incarcerated veterans. In doing so, it would include an area in which to honor his father—a military hero himself. A noble idea, but Barbara and I didn't think it a feasible plan. It seems to me that Bill has found the perfect way to not reimburse me for the large expenses that I covered over the years. Time will tell.

Barbara, caretaker Bob, and I worked to sell some garden items like antique iron gates, stone lions, tall stone figurines, and smaller garden items. Barbara was also successful in changing the ownership of two life insurance policies owned by Bill's dad, Bill being the insured. Doing so settled a line of credit left by Bill's mom that I'd been paying down. Other monies were used to discharge an outstanding storage unit bill and obtain new liability insurance on the house. We compensated the gardener who removed vegetation to help fireproof the property.

Yes, my family thought I was foolish to be involved with this process, but Barbara needed my help. She only became involved with the trust management in late 2022/early 2023, and she hadn't known the history of the house and the relationship problems. When she'd agreed to step in, it was during a difficult time for everyone. She appreciated my moral support as she navigated some of the issues and tried to communicate with Bill.

Barbara's 8-13-23 text to me: "I told him that you'd really been helpful."

Barbara's 1-14-24 text to me: "I hope you are rewarded for such goodwill acts 100,000,000-fold."

The house still sits unoccupied. Barbara hoped to clear out all the stuff and list it for sale in the spring of 2024. Bill still thinks I have a lien on the house and certain possessions that are there or in storage. Most of what's there are books, his family heirlooms, his writings, and various keepsakes. He even thinks that I want to claim his property and possessions outside the US. But I've never had proof of their existence, and I've never entertained such plans.

Barbara saw Bill again in early February 2024 and extended the six-month deadline to the end of April. She told me in a phone conversation that he had texted that his plan would be resolved in two months. She also said that she planned to revisit Bill in late March. One of the things to discuss would be the money I feel is owed to me by the trust.

In preparation for that meeting, I presented my claim to Barbara and the trust's current attorney, Lance Brown. Lance suggested that I speak with another attorney as he couldn't advise me since he represents the trust. I spoke with one attorney briefly who said that Barbara would have to agree with me filing a lien on the house. She could present my dollar amount to Bill, but if he didn't agree and she paid me anyway (when funds were available) he could sue her for not acting responsibly as the trustee. We could then see if he would agree to a lesser amount. If I decided to go to court over the matter, a judge could disallow any of my payments over two to three years old, which is the bulk of the amount.

I was so enraged after that phone conversation. Once again, I realized how difficult it is to fully untangle oneself from a narcissist's hold.

June 2024: It seems that the issue of the house and reimbursement to me is being resolved. There is a plan in place for Bill's trust to donate the house to the non-profit mentioned earlier. They plan to sell it to purchase a property that is more suitable for their purposes of helping veterans. Once the house is sold, I am to finally be paid. Time will tell. Stay tuned to find out the results.

* * *

Is there life after being with the narcissist? Yes!

Do I regret that it took me so long to wake up, see what was happening in our relationship, and do something about it? Yes!

Have I learned valuable lessons along the way? Yes!

Do I have a much better understanding of what I want for myself?

Yes!

Am I willing to show my vulnerability and share my insights with others? Yes!

Like all of my other ex-husbands, Bill was definitely a teacher for me. The biggest lesson I learned from our marriage (and the previous six) was the importance of taking care of myself. Putting myself first for a change was not selfish. It was healthy.

I find myself much happier with my life and myself in general, I'm taking much better care of myself. I've lost weight without lectures and without extreme efforts. The change has been noticed and I'm getting lots of compliments.

Another thing I'm doing is participating in activities that sing to my soul. For example, I schedule monthly massages. I read a lot. I walk almost daily in my beautiful neighborhood. All I have to do is walk out my door, and I'm in nature. I'm also meeting new people who have had similar experiences, making me realize that I'm not alone.

I receive valuable counsel from my spirit guides. Their wisdom, insights, and encouragement are things I will forever be grateful for. They have comforted me through some very dark moments in these last three years and have seen me grow to new heights. They also remind me about who I truly am. When walking, I often receive inspiration from them for my writing or an upcoming talk for which I'm preparing.

I have done my inner work and will continue to do so. Therapy has been very beneficial even after the divorce became final. My therapist reminds me of the progress I've made. It's good to have someone other than family to check in with as she looks at my situation without familial attachment and the need to protect me. It takes a long time to break ingrained patterns and learn to function differently. Therapy helps me with that.

During my healing journey, I was uplifted by Glennon Doyle's book *Untamed*. She wrote that heartbreak is one of the greatest clues of our lives, and that when it rings, it's up to us to answer the door. She also wrote, "The thing that breaks your heart is the very thing you were born to help heal. Every world changer's work begins with a broken heart." I know heartbreak, and I choose to rise above it.

I want to help others who find themselves in toxic relationships. To do so, I've been sharing my experiences and lessons learned by speaking on podcasts. I also plan to find other speaking opportunities like summits, retreats, and conferences. I plan to form healing groups for peer support. I am creating a healing journal as a companion piece to this book. I really enjoy public speaking, as it's empowering to have found my voice and not be afraid to speak my truth.

Who knows? Maybe there's a comedy routine waiting to be debuted because I refuse to wallow in the pain.

What are my plans now that I'm divorced? I may be almost seventy, but I'm not dead yet, as my daughter reminds me often. I have lots to do. Here's what my bucket list includes:

- Retiring from bookkeeping
- Traveling
- Making new friends

- Facilitating a healing group
- Dancing
- Being a "grandma" for hospitalized children
- Continuing my self-improvement
- Continually deepening my relationship with my daughter
- Knitting, reading, and walking more often
- Writing more books

Will there be romance in my future? Who knows. I'm hoping so. It would be wonderful to meet the one with whom I can have a healthy, loving relationship. In addition to sharing common interests, the ability to discuss intense topics, be flexible, and compromise are important to me. Experience has taught me the value of taking as much time as I need to see if the other person and I are well-suited.

One thing is certain: Life is messy. I've learned from my mistakes, and now I'm making better choices. I couldn't be happier. It took me fifty years, but I have my life back. I see myself as loveable, wonderful, and "enough" just the way I am. I'm looking forward to new adventures and lots of fun. I survived the roller coaster ride of marriage with a narcissist, and now I'm thriving!

Sign up for Jo Ann's email list and receive the poster, "Red Flags of Narcissistic Abuse."

https://joannfawcett.com

ABOUT THE AUTHOR

 Jo Ann Fawcett is a California native. She has Associate of Arts degrees in film production and Accounting. She is the mother of a successful grown daughter and is the proud grandmother of three. She enjoys reading, needlework, walking, traveling, and spending time with the family. She is owned by her cat Winston.

Jo Ann never aspired to be a writer. In the late 90s, she published a community newspaper, writing articles about interesting places to visit and environmental issues. Years later while speaking at a Super Soldier conference about her former husband's military experiences, an attendee asked her when her next story was coming out. Not her husband's next story – HER story. Several years later, Jo Ann finally put her story on paper.

Jo Ann writes from the heart and is grateful for the inspiration that flows to her. She writes matter-of-factly, weaving in her own style of humor. She openly shares her vulnerability. Readers enjoy her honesty and praise her courage to share her story. Through her many struggles, she found her strengths, gifts, and inner power. She learned that dreams can, and do, come true. Today she is a warrior who proudly carries the title, Wise Woman-Crone. Midlife Magic is Jo Ann's first book. The memoir contains stories about her first six marriages involving abuse, divorce, and death. Jo Ann talks about meeting and marrying husband #7, a former military intelligence officer incarcerated for a crime he didn't commit. Having been an active member of the Mormon Church for nearly 30 years, Jo Ann left the Church to fully embrace the world of UFOs, elementals, magic, and the paranormal – a new path she loves.

The Prince Was Wrong – Leaving the Narcissist Behind is Jo Ann's second book. This book is a follow-up memoir to the first book as Jo Ann discovered the reality that her husband #7 is a narcissist. This book discusses the red flags of this type of abuse. It lays out the demise of their relationship with clear examples of his narcissistic behavior. The 'happy ending' chapter shows that Jo Ann has found a joyous life after divorcing #7 and is on the path to creating her best life.

The magical benefit of writing these books and doing her healing inner work is that Jo Ann has found her voice, passion, and desire to help other women who feel stuck and overwhelmed in their toxic relationships. Jo Ann wishes to offer the hope that healing can happen. Their lives can get better. They can find peace and joy in their lives once again.

LinkedIn
https://www.linkedin.com/in/jo-ann-fawcett-a7b9b832/
Facebook
https://www.facebook.com/jo.a.richards.5
Instagram
https://www.instagram.com/jo.ann.fawcett.author/
Website
www.joannfawcett.com